RE

Teen
World

Multi-level photocopiable activities for teenagers

Joanna Budden

CAMBRIDGE
UNIVERSITY PRESS

CAMBRIDGE UNIVERSITY PRESS
Cambridge, New York, Melbourne, Madrid, Cape Town, Singapore, São Paulo, Delhi

Cambridge University Press
The Edinburgh Building, Cambridge CB2 8RU, UK

www.cambridge.org
Information on this title: www.cambridge.org/9780521721554

First published 2009

Printed in the United Kingdom by Polestar Wheatons Ltd., Exeter

A catalogue record for this publication is available from the British Library

ISBN 978-0-521-72155-4

Contents

Map of the book 4

Introduction 7

1 Welcome to English 9
2 Technology 16
3 Music 22
4 Work and money 28
5 Humour 34
6 Appearances 40
7 Crime and justice 46
8 Heroes and heroines 52
9 Sport 58
10 Consumer society 64
11 Ambitions and hopes 70
12 Media and news 76
13 Relationships 82
14 Television and film 88
15 Age and the future 94
16 Travel 100
17 The environment 106

Thanks and acknowledgements inside back cover

Map of the book

Unit	Title	Level	Language focus	Skills focus	Activity type
1 Welcome to English	1.1 Cross the classroom	elementary	functional classroom language	speaking: asking questions	board game
	1.2 New term resolutions	intermediate	strengths and weaknesses	reading: information gap writing: resolutions	walking dictation
	1.3 Dictionary dive	upper-intermediate	word definitions, parts of speech	writing: definitions	word game
2 Technology	2.1 Teenspace	elementary	personal information, likes and dislikes	writing: profiles reading: gist	making a web page
	2.2 Chat room	intermediate	question forms	writing and reading: messages, error correction	group writing activity
	2.3 Virtual worlds	upper-intermediate	modals for speculating	speaking: speculating writing: description	matching activity
3 Music	3.1 Musical postcards	elementary	past simple	writing: a postcard reading: skimming	group drawing activity, writing a postcard
	3.2 Music fans	intermediate	question forms	speaking: asking questions writing: summarising	questionnaire
	3.3 Music festival	upper-intermediate	making suggestions, giving opinions	speaking: discussing, presenting	planning a festival
4 Work and money	4.1 Workbusters	elementary	relative pronouns, jobs, prices	speaking: pronunciation, answering questions	team game
	4.2 Holiday jobs	intermediate	modal verbs, question forms	speaking: asking and answering questions	role-play
	4.3 Are you money mad?	upper-intermediate	giving opinions, money vocabulary	reading: answering questions speaking: discussing	questionnaire
5 Humour	5.1 Funny comic	elementary	direct speech	speaking and writing: storytelling	writing a comic
	5.2 Bad jokes	intermediate	questions	reading: matching speaking: telling jokes	jokes
	5.3 Watch out! There's a joker about!	upper-intermediate	present tenses	reading and speaking: ranking writing: practical jokes	planning a TV programme
6 Appearances	6.1 Extreme makeover	elementary	present simple, present continuous, clothes	speaking and writing: discussing, describing	describing people
	6.2 Teen tribes	intermediate	present simple, present continuous, clothes	reading: matching speaking: discussing	matching activity discussion
	6.3 Inside-out or not at all?	upper-intermediate	questions, second conditional	reading: answering questions speaking: discussing	questionnaire

Unit	Title	Level	Language focus	Skills focus	Activity type
7 Crime and justice	7.1 School alibi	elementary	question forms, past continuous, past simple	speaking: asking and answering questions	role-play
7 Crime and justice	7.2 Dodgy dilemmas	intermediate	past continuous, past simple, *should*	speaking: making excuses	role-play
7 Crime and justice	7.3 Crime controversy	upper-intermediate	relative clauses, present simple, crime	reading: answering questions speaking: describing, persuading	word game questionnaire
8 Heroes and heroines	8.1 Superhero comic	elementary	*can* for ability, direct speech	writing: storytelling	making a comic
8 Heroes and heroines	8.2 Heroic sketches	intermediate	narrative tenses	writing: storytelling	writing and performing a sketch
8 Heroes and heroines	8.3 Real-life heroes	upper-intermediate	present simple, conditionals, *should*, jobs	speaking: justifying, persuading	debate
9 Sport	9.1 Footie stars	elementary	comparatives, question forms	speaking: asking questions, comparing	card game
9 Sport	9.2 Sports reporters	intermediate	question forms	speaking: asking and answering questions, summarising	interviews
9 Sport	9.3 Sports quiz	upper-intermediate	questions, sports	speaking: answering questions	quiz
10 Consumer society	10.1 Shopping spree	elementary	functional shopping language	speaking: asking for things	role-play
10 Consumer society	10.2 The real cost	intermediate	present simple and past simple passives	speaking: discussing	matching activity, discussion
10 Consumer society	10.3 Buy Nothing Day	upper-intermediate	tense revision, relative clauses	reading: understanding main ideas speaking: speculating	reading an article and exchanging ideas
11 Ambitions and hopes	11.1 Nervous Nathan's diary	elementary	past simple, future simple	reading: extracting key information writing: a blog	reading, writing a blog
11 Ambitions and hopes	11.2 How ambitious are you?	intermediate	questions	reading: answering questions speaking: agreeing and disagreeing	questionnaire
11 Ambitions and hopes	11.3 Thinking time	upper-intermediate	future tenses, present simple	speaking and writing: sharing information	discussion
12 Media and news	12.1 Newsite	elementary	present simple, present continuous, *going to*, past simple, future simple	reading: understanding main ideas writing: news reports	reading, making a web page
12 Media and news	12.2 Paparazzi pyramid	intermediate	giving opinions	speaking: agreeing and disagreeing, fluency	discussion
12 Media and news	12.3 TV news competition	upper-intermediate	language of news broadcasts	writing and speaking: presenting information	making a news programme

	Title	Level	Language focus	Skills focus	Activity type
13 Relationships	13.1 Family match	elementary	question forms, present simple, possessive *'s*, family vocabulary	speaking: asking and answering questions	card game
	13.2 In your parents' shoes	intermediate	past simple, past continuous, language of persuasion	speaking: explaining, persuading	role-play
	13.3 A problem shared ...	upper-intermediate	modal verbs	speaking: asking for and giving advice	role-play
14 TV and film	14.1 Square eyes	elementary	question forms, present simple, past simple	speaking: asking and answering questions writing: note taking	questionnaire
	14.2 Murder of the movie maker	intermediate	present simple, present continuous, films	speaking and writing: planning a movie	planning a movie
	14.3 Reality TV show	upper-intermediate	colloquial expressions	speaking: interacting	role-play
15 Age and the future	15.1 Fortune teller	elementary	*will* for predictions	speaking: asking questions, making predictions	making a fortune teller
	15.2 Vote for me	intermediate	first conditional	writing: targeting an audience speaking: persuading	making a poster, giving a speech
	15.3 The walk of life	upper-intermediate	tense revision	speaking: expressing opinions	a board game
16 Travel	16.1 Get the message across	elementary	functional travel language	speaking: explaining writing: a dialogue	game, role-play
	16.2 English abroad	intermediate	agreeing and disagreeing, *would*, travel	reading: extracing key information speaking: discussing	discussion
	16.3 Gap year blog	upper-intermediate	mixed conditionals	reading: understanding main ideas speaking: discussing writing: a blog	reading, a blog
17 The environment	17.1 Recycling race	elementary	singular and plural forms, materials	speaking: giving information	board game
	17.2 Ecological footprint	intermediate	adverbs of frequency	reading: answering questions speaking: comparing	questionnaire
	17.3 Car ban	upper-intermediate	giving opinions	reading: extracting key information speaking: persuading	role-play

Introduction

What is *Teen World*?

Teen World is a photocopiable resource book designed to give teenage students the opportunity to communicate with one another in meaningful and enjoyable ways. Each task has been designed especially with teenagers in mind.

Who is *Teen World* for?

Teen World is for teachers of English whose students are aged 11–18 and who want to introduce their students to topics that will interest and engage them. This is not to say that teachers will not find many of the activities useful with other age groups, but the book has been primarily written for teens. This book can be used to supplement any course book material or to provide self-contained topic-based lessons. The activities are clear and simple to use, with minimal preparation required.

How is *Teen World* organised?

Teen World is divided into 17 units, each focusing on a different topic of interest to teenagers. Each unit provides one activity for the following levels: elementary, intermediate and upper-intermediate.

The Map of the book and the focus boxes at the start of each activity give information as to which lexical, grammatical and skill areas are covered. This allows easy integration into your syllabus. With each activity, step-by-step instructions are given, as well as an indication of how much preparation and class time the activity should take.

What types of activity are in *Teen World*?

Teen World includes a wide variety of activity types which will keep your students engaged and on-task as they develop their language skills within the topic areas. Although all skills are covered within the book, the focus is very much on speaking activities and encouraging real communication between students, whether in groups or pairs, and also between the students and the teacher. The activities are motivating and meaningful and give your students a reason for communicating. Activity types include board games, role-plays, quizzes and surveys.

How is each activity organised?

Each activity offers the teacher a warm-up task to lead into the main activity and several suggestions for follow-up activities. The main activity is explained clearly and simply, guiding you through the stages of the lesson. The follow-up activities can often be used as short fillers to round off the class, or, if you have time available to develop them, some can be used to lead into more extensive project work on the topic. However, as with any lesson plan in any teacher's book, do adapt the activities to your students and to best suit your own teaching style and context.

How can I get the most out of *Teen World*?

Many of the activities in *Teen World* are excellent starting points for exploring new topics with your class. The teacher's notes offer you ideas in the follow-up tasks on how to extend the activities and some of the tasks lend themselves to developing mini projects. Some follow-up tasks may offer the opportunity of localising the task, bringing it closer to home and thinking about the topic within the backdrop of the students' own town or city, or personalising the activity, which will also give you the opportunity to get to know your students better.

How do the activities develop communicative skills?

As students carry out the activities they revise specific grammar points and lexical sets. They also extend their vocabulary as they explore new topic areas. The new vocabulary they learn during the activities is useful and relevant to what they are doing and therefore will be memorable. As well as expanding students' vocabulary and revising grammar, many of the activities in *Teen World* have been designed to give students the opportunity to express their opinions and feelings towards an issue within a topic; teenagers often respond very well to the opportunity to express their views and to explore their ideas on issues that interest and affect them.

Recycling new vocabulary

It is always a good idea to recycle new vocabulary regularly, and within *Teen World* there are plenty of opportunities for students to increase their vocabulary within the topic areas. As well as being introduced to new words, students will need to revise and recycle language regularly. The following are suggestions of how to recycle and revise vocabulary in fun ways:

- Write down all the new words students have learnt in a lesson on cards and keep them in a special 'word bag' or envelope so you can regularly recycle them.
- Put a word card on each student's chair. As they arrive in the class, they have to say a sentence including the word before they can sit down.
- Put students into pairs and give each pair four or five words that they have learnt. Ask students to create a dialogue incorporating at least three of the words.
- Divide the class into teams. Ask one person from each team to sit at the front of the class with their back to the board. Write a word students have learnt on the board. Each team has to describe the word to the person at the front of the class. The first to get the word gets a point. Award extra points for good definitions.

Managing the activities

If some of the activity types in *Teen World* are new to your students, ensure adequate time is given in explaining and demonstrating the activity before the students begin. As students are doing the activity, be sure to monitor carefully and be available to offer advice and to feed in new language as and when required. Remind students that the process is just as important as the end product (if there is one) and that you are watching throughout the whole task to see who is making a real effort. Effort in speaking English, collaborating with classmates and using initiative should be praised and rewarded throughout each activity.

Classroom dynamics

The activities in *Teen World* offer the perfect opportunity for you to get to know your students better and for them to get to know one another. Students frequently have the chance to work in pairs and small groups. In most cases I suggest you mix up the groupings regularly so that students work with a variety of different people. However you decide to group your students, this should be taken into consideration at the planning stage. You may decide to put students into friendship groups for some of the activities or you may like to pair up weak and strong students or students of similar levels for certain activities.

Cross the classroom

Language focus
functional classroom language practice

Key vocabulary
functional classroom language and classroom items:
book, coloured pencil, folder, homework, pen, pencil, pencil sharpener, rubber

Skills focus
speaking: asking questions using functional classroom language

Level
elementary

Time
60 minutes

Preparation
for the warm-up – one enlarged set of picture cards and speech bubbles (on card if possible) to use with the whole class; blu-tak; one set of cards, cut up, and one photocopy of the board game and a coin for each group of 3 or 4 students, a counter for each student (or they could use a paperclip, sharpener or rubber)

Extra notes
By spending some time revising useful language at the beginning of a new term, we remind our students that we expect them to use English whenever possible.

Warm-up

1. Show students your enlarged picture cards one by one and ask them to guess what classroom language each represents. They may come up with slight variations to what is in the speech bubbles and that's fine. Stick the picture cards on the board so everyone can see.
2. Now show the speech bubbles one by one and ask for volunteers to come up, read them out and stick them next to the corresponding picture card.
3. Give students the chance to practise saying the language by doing some snappy choral drilling. Model the language and ask students to repeat after you.

Main activity

1. It is important to do the warm-up before the main activity. Put students into groups of three or four and give each group a copy of the board game (page 11), a set of cards (page 10) and a coin. Each student will also need a counter.
2. The aim of the game is to move from the classroom door to the board. Students can choose their route through the board. However, to add an extra challenge, the rule is that students can't move onto a circle if another player is already on it. They have to go around them. Only one player at a time can be on each circle.
3. Instead of using a dice, students toss a coin. If they get 'heads' they can move two spaces, 'tails' one space. Students should look at the picture they land on and make a full sentence connected to it. For example, if they land on the pencil sharpener, they should say: *Can I borrow a pencil sharpener, please?* or *Do you have a pencil sharpener?* or *How do you say* (pencil sharpener in their language) *in English*? The other group members should decide if the sentence is valid or not. If it is not valid, they must move back to where they came from.
4. If a player lands on a Team question circle, the player on their right should ask them a question related to classroom language. For example: *What do you say if you forget your homework?* or *What's this in English?* (pointing to something in the classroom). Write on the board *What do you say if …?* as a model. The player must answer correctly, or move back.
5. If a player lands on a 'Take a card' circle, they should turn over one of the cards. If it is a word card, they should translate it into their own language. If it is a picture card, they should say the sentence it represents.
6. The winner is the first person in each team to reach the board.

Follow-up

- Put students into groups of three or four and give each group a set of cards from Part 1 to play 'Pelmanism':
  - Place all the cards face down on the table in random order.
  - Player 1 turns over two cards and reads the words on each card or says the words the picture represents. If the cards match, Player 1 keeps the cards. If they don't match, Player 1 puts them back in the same place, face down.
  - The next player has a turn. Play until there are no cards left. The winner is the person with the most matching pairs.
- Make classroom language speech bubbles to display around the classroom.
  If the classroom language that you expect your students to use during the class is visible in the room, it is easy for you to encourage its use by simply pointing to the correct speech bubble when the students make mistakes or use their own language.

1.1 Cross the classroom

Cards

I'm sorry I'm late.	Can I borrow a … please?	I'm sorry. I've forgotten my …
How long do we have to do this?	Have you finished? Yes, I've finished. No, I haven't finished.	Can I go to the toilet, please?
Sorry, but I don't understand.	Could you repeat the instructions, please?	How do you say … in English?

HOMEWORK
TEN MINUTES
YES
NO
?
INSTRUCTIONS
?
TELEPHONE
?

1.1 Cross the classroom

Board game

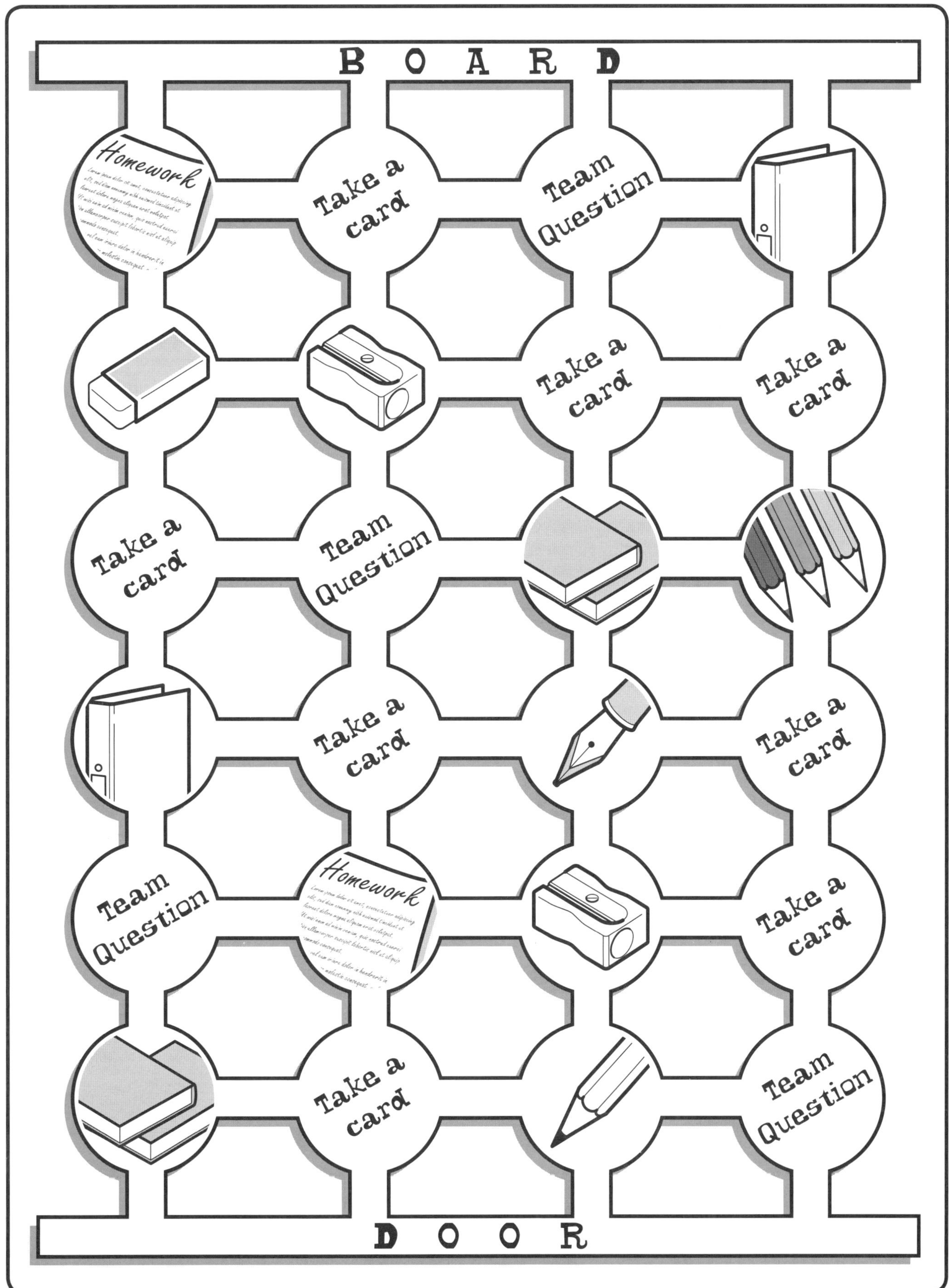
BOARD
Homework
Take a card
Team Question
Take a card
Take a card
Take a card
Team Question
Take a card
Take a card
Team Question
Homework
Take a card
Take a card
Team Question
DOOR

New term resolutions

Language focus
expressing personal strengths, weaknesses and preferences; *will* for decisions

Key vocabulary
activity, favourite, I'm (not) good at … , the best/worst thing …

Skills focus
reading, dictating and writing: resolutions

Level
intermediate

Time
60 minutes

Preparation
one photocopy for each student and one photocopy (enlarged and cut up) of the sentence beginnings at the bottom of this page

Extra notes
This activity is designed to be used near the beginning of a course or a new term with a new group of students. It gives you the chance to find out how they feel about learning English, what types of activity they enjoy and what they consider to be their strengths and weaknesses of language learning.

Warm-up

- Write on the board ENGLISH CLASS and ask your students to connect as many relevant words as they can in the form of a crossword so there are interlinking words. Whoever links the most words in a set time wins.

Main activity

1. Stick the enlarged dictation sentence beginnings (see bottom of this page) on the wall around different parts of the classroom.
2. Put students into pairs of 'walker' and 'writer'. The 'walker' has to go to each of the dictation strips in turn, read it, remember it, return to their partner and dictate the sentence to them. Their partner has to write it on their activity sheet in the corresponding space. Tell students to make sure that the sentence numbers correspond.
3. Give each student an activity sheet and tell them that these must stay on the desks at all times. 'Walkers' must not take the sheets with them and they must not shout to their partners from across the room.
4. Set a time limit and ensure all students start at the same time if you are planning to have a class race. If you wish, halfway through the activity students can change roles, and the 'walkers' become the 'writers'.
5. Check that all students have written all six sentence beginnings and then ask them to complete the sentences so they are true for them. Ask for some examples to ensure all students are on track. For example:
   *In English I'm very good at **reading and learning new vocabulary.***
6. Ask students if they have ever made 'New Year's resolutions' at the beginning of a new year and listen to some of their examples or share some that you have made in the past. Now ask your students to think of a 'New Term resolution' for the English class. Give some examples, but encourage students to think for a minute about themselves and their learning before they write their resolution and sign it. Examples could be:
   I will try to do all my English homework this term or *I will listen when the teacher is explaining the activities* or *I will try to talk only in English.*
7. At the bottom of the resolution there's a space for the teacher or student to add a signature at the end of the term if the resolution was achieved.

Follow-up

- Collect in the answer sheets and try to respond to some students' comments in future classes by incorporating some of their favourite activity types or working in a supportive way on areas that they find difficult.
- Display students' resolutions on group posters round the classroom as a constant reminder of their New term resolutions.

✂

1	In English I'm very good at …	4	For me, the best thing about English is …
2	In English I'm not very good at …	5	My favourite activities in the English class are …
3	For me, the worst thing about English is …	6	In the future I think English is going to be …

1.2 New term resolutions

Name:

1. In ____________ ________ very ________ ________

....

2. ________ ____________ ________ not ________ good ________

....

3. ________ me, ________ worst ________ about ____________ ________

....

4. For ________ , ________ ________ thing ________ English ________

....

5. My ____________ activities ________ ________ ____________ ________ are

....

6. In ______ ________ _____ ________ ________ _____ going _____ _____

....

✂- -

My 'new term resolution' for this English class is:

____

____

____

Signed ____

Achieved on (date): ____________________________

Signed ____

Dictionary dive

Language focus
dictionary definitions

Key vocabulary
parts of speech: *noun, verb, adjective, adverb*

Skills focus
using a dictionary and becoming familiar with the style of dictionary definitions; speaking: sounding convincing writing: definitions

Level
upper-intermediate

Time
45 minutes

Preparation
one set of cards per class; access to dictionaries, preferably monolingual; two or three blank cards per small group

Warm-up

- If you have a class set of dictionaries, distribute them amongst your students so everyone can see one, and have a quick dictionary quiz. Ask questions to get your students using the dictionary and looking up words. For example:
Where can you find a list of the phonemic symbols?
What word comes straight after 'cauldron'?
What information do you get next to a word, apart from its definition?
How do you pronounce the word 'mischievous' and what does it mean? (Write the word up on the board, don't say it out loud! Get students to look up the word and use the phonemic script to get the correct pronunciation.)

Main activity

1. This activity is based on a popular word game. The idea of the game is for participants to create fictitious definitions for words and try to trick their opponents into believing the invented, rather than the real, definition.
2. Before you begin, demonstrate the game using the word 'bamboozle'. Read the three definitions convincingly and ask students to vote on the correct definition. (The correct answer is underlined.)

WORD bamboozle

Definition 1 *verb.* (informal) To trick or deceive someone often by giving them confusing information. E.g. She was bamboozled into revealing her credit card number.

Definition 2 *noun.* A person with a short concentration span. E.g. Weren't you listening? You're such a bamboozle!

Definition 3 *verb.* To walk slowly, without a final objective. E.g. She loves bamboozling around the town centre.

3. Divide the class into pairs or small groups and give each group a definition card or two (depending on your class size). Give them time to write two false definitions in the spaces. As they do this, monitor carefully and help students to write definitions that sound like they have come from a real dictionary.
4. Groups take it in turns to read out their definitions to the class convincingly and keeping a straight face.
5. Award points to the teams who guess the definitions correctly.
6. After this round, give students some blank cards. In groups students should create two or three definition cards. They should look through a dictionary to find words they think may be useful or interesting to present to the class. Using the dictionary for the real definition, and their imaginations for the two false definitions, you will have enough cards to play another round of the game.

Follow-up

- If you have Internet access in your classroom, show students some examples of online dictionaries. The definitions for this activity have been adapted from the Cambridge online dictionary: http://dictionary.cambridge.org/
- Students write a list of top tips for using a dictionary.

1.3 Dictionary dive

WORD scrimp /skrɪmp/

Definition 1: ....

Definition 2: *verb.* To save money by spending less than necessary. E.g. *Don't travel on FLYFREE airlines, they **scrimp** on security!*

Definition 3: ....

WORD doodle /duː.dl/

Definition 1: *verb.* To draw pictures or patterns when you're bored or distracted. E.g. *He was **doodling** during the English class!*

Definition 2: ....

Definition 3: ....

WORD gadget /gædʒ.ɪt/

Definition 1: ....

Definition 2: ....

Definition 3: *noun.* A small device or machine with a specific purpose. E.g. *I've just bought a new **gadget** for cleaning my keyboard.*

WORD chuffed /tʃʌft/

Definition 1: ....

Definition 2: *adjective.* (informal) Pleased or happy. E.g. *He was **chuffed** she asked him out.*

Definition 3: ....

WORD tickle /tɪk.l/

Definition 1: *verb.* To touch someone lightly with your fingers, often making them laugh. E.g. *Stop **tickling** me!*

Definition 2: ....

Definition 3: ....

WORD whinge /wɪndʒ/

Definition 1: ....

Definition 2: ....

Definition 3: *verb.* To complain about something that doesn't seem important. E.g. *Will you stop **whinging**, please!*

WORD spotless /spɒt.ləs/

Definition 1: *adjective.* Extremely clean. E.g. *The house was **spotless**.*

Definition 2: ....

Definition 3: ....

WORD dimwit /dɪm.wɪt/

Definition 1: ....

Definition 2: *noun.* A stupid person. E.g. *Oh no, I forgot my book again, I'm such a **dimwit**!*

Definition 3: ....

WORD hullabaloo /hʌl.ə.bəluː/

Definition 1: ....

Definition 2: ....

Definition 3: *noun.* (old fashioned) A loud noise made by angry people. E.g. *The protesters were making a real **hullabaloo**.*

WORD wanderlust /wɒn.də.lʌst/

Definition 1: *noun.* The desire to travel far away and to many different places. E.g. *Everyone's full of **wanderlust** in the summer.*

Definition 2: ....

Definition 3: ....

Teenspace

Language focus
giving personal details; *love / hate / don't mind* + gerund

Key vocabulary
ambition, favourite thing, future, graffiti wall, hobby, message board, status, wish (noun), *worry* (noun)

Skills focus
writing and reading personal profiles and writing comments in response to them

Level
elementary

Time
40 minutes + an optional 5 or 10 minutes per class for the next 3 or 4 classes

Preparation
one photocopy for each student, enlarged to A3 size if possible; sticky notes or labels for students to update their 'status' in future classes. Try to have a look at *Facebook* and *MySpace* on the Internet before the class, if you are unfamiliar with this type of website.

Extra notes
This activity can also be used successfully for higher levels as most of the language is student generated.

Warm-up

1. Write on the board THE INTERNET (or play a quick game of Hangman to get it on the board). Then ask students what they think about when they think of the Internet and write their ideas around the main word like a mind map. They may suggest some of the following: WWW (world wide web), email, chat rooms, shopping, messenger, blogs, personal web pages, etc.
2. Whether or not it's mentioned, ask students about any personal web pages they may have or know about such as *MySpace* or *Facebook*. Even if these sites are new to you, you may well find that your teenage students are familiar with them, and if they are, try to use the natural information gap between you and them to find out as much as you can from your students.

Main activity

1. Give each student a copy of the activity sheet. Ask them to bring in a photograph or a picture to stick on the page for the next class. It doesn't have to be a photo of themselves; it could be a picture that shows something they love or anything that will represent them.
2. Ask students to complete the personal information (name, birthday, etc.). The 'Status' section is for them to put how they're feeling at that moment. For example, *Janet is tired because she went to a party last night* or *Pablo is happy because it's his birthday tomorrow.*
3. Next, students fill in the Personal info and Favourites sections. When these sections are completed you can display the Teenspace profiles on the classroom wall or, if that isn't practical, put students into groups of six or seven and they can pass the profiles around the group. The students should read their classmates' profiles. If they want to write a comment or a question, they should do this on the 'message board'. If they want to draw a picture or make a statement, they can do this on the 'graffiti wall'.
4. The Teenspace profiles should be as flexible and interactive as possible. If you have space to leave them displayed on the wall, in a future class you can give students a sticky note or sticky label and ask them to update their profile. They should stick their new status over their old one. Give students time to read each others' profiles and write messages and comments on them. This can be an on-going activity until the pages are full up or the students have tired of the task.
5. When the Teenspace profiles are complete, ask students whose pages look like the most interesting sites. You could have a class vote to choose the most original or detailed page.

Follow-up

- Repeat the task, but instead of students using their own personal details they could choose a famous person to be.
- Ask students to think of some new applications they would like to add to their page too. Ideas to get them going could be interactive games of chess, photo share areas, quizzes, puzzles, etc.
- Use the information from the pages to create a class quiz about your students.

2.1 Teenspace

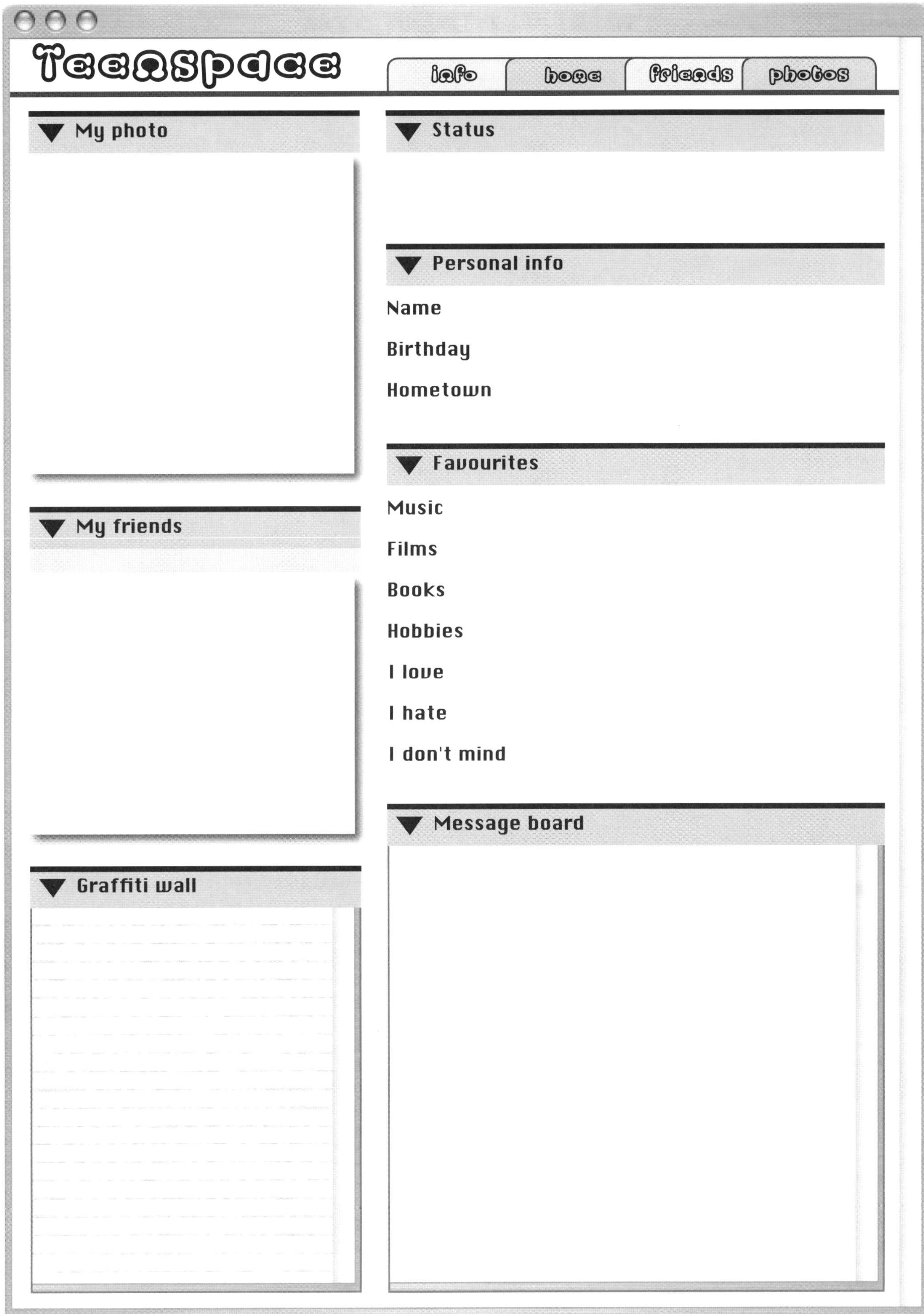

Teenspace
info
home
friends
photos
My photo
Status
Personal info
Name
Birthday
Hometown
Favourites
Music
Films
Books
Hobbies
I love
I hate
I don't mind
My friends
Graffiti wall
Message board

Chat room

Language focus
question forms

Key vocabulary
getting to know people (student generated)

Skills focus
writing and reading chat room messages; error correction

Level
intermediate

Time
60 minutes

Preparation
one photocopy for each student

Warm-up

1. Ask your students if they ever use Internet chat rooms. If so, ask them some general questions like who they chat to and what they chat about.
2. Ask them if they have 'nicknames' for chatting online. If so, they can use them for this activity; otherwise ask them to invent a nickname.

Main activity

1. Tell your students they are going to take part in a crazy chat room. If at all possible, students should move their chairs into a circle for this activity.
2. Explain to students that *you* are going to take the role of the Internet server and stand in the middle of the circle. When students are ready to 'send' their messages, they should hold up their paper so you can see who is ready. You then pass it to someone who is waiting to receive a message.
3. Give all the chat room participants (the rest of the class) a copy of the activity sheet. When the chat begins, they can write anything they like, within reason. They should always write their nickname before they begin their message. Tell them that the Internet server has a 'Super Scout' system that will destroy any papers from chatters who send inappropriate messages.
4. As soon as students finish a message they should hold their paper up in the air so the net (you!) can pick up their paper and give it to *any* student who also has a message ready to send. As mentioned above, as you exchange the messages you should glance at the papers to check for anything inappropriate.
5. When the activity is in progress it becomes faster and quite exciting as the papers are flying around the room and the chat is growing. Let the chat go on for about ten or fifteen minutes or until the first chat paper is completed, then the Internet crashes.
6. Now the papers should be returned to the people who started each chat. Ask a few students to read out their chat conversation to the class. The results will often be amusing for all to hear.
7. Then ask students what tools we have on computers to check for our mistakes. We usually always have a grammar- and spelling-check tool. But, of course, in our crazy chat room we didn't have these tools, so ask the students to read the chats carefully and to find the top five mistakes. These mistakes should be ones that students should know how to correct themselves, and which have been made because they were writing quickly. Mistakes that were made because students were trying to use language beyond their level don't need to be corrected now.
8. When the whole group has completed their top five mistakes, ask students for group feedback and collate a class list of the top ten mistakes. These could be used for a mini progress check in a future class.

Follow-up

- If you have access to a computer room, you could progress from this paper-based chat to a real chat room. Ensure that the online space you choose is a safe one for teenagers.
- Making e-pals with a class of English language students from another school, city or preferably another country can be a great way to motivate teenagers and get them writing in English.

2.2 Chat room

Teens chat

Top five chat mistakes

Have a look at the chat you and your cybermates have written. Can you find any mistakes? Choose five mistakes and correct them.

	Mistake	Correction
1		
2		
3		
4		
5		

Virtual worlds

Language focus
modal verbs for speculating: *could be, must be, might be, may be*, etc.

Key vocabulary
virtual worlds: *avatar, business, escapism, fantasy character, island, personality*

Skills focus
speaking: speculating; writing a description of an imagined person

Level
upper-intermediate

Time
60 minutes

Preparation
one photocopy, cut up, for every pair or group of 3 students.
If virtual worlds and *Second Life* are new to you and/or your students, take a look at the *Second Life* website.

Warm-up

1. Say:
Yesterday evening I met some friends and we went swimming with dolphins. Then we looked around an art gallery and went shopping. I bought a new necklace and changed my hair colour from blue to pink!
2. Ask students to guess how you had such an eventful evening! Encourage them to ask you questions until they guess you were inside a virtual world such as *Second Life.*
3. Ask students what they know about virtual worlds. If your students know more about virtual worlds than you do, use the natural information gap between you and them to generate discussion.

Main activity

1. Put students into pairs or small groups and give them a copy of Part 1. Ask them to match the four pictures of 'avatars' (characters within virtual worlds) with the four photographs. They should try and justify their guesses. Tell students to trust their instincts and to rely on their first impressions. The idea is to get students to speculate. Ask students if they think people try to reflect their true personalities when they create their *Second Life* avatars. Discuss this with your students.
2. Now give each pair or group a copy of Part 2. Ask them to read each text and to speculate which two of the people in the Part 1 photos might have written it. (The abbreviation SL = Second Life, and RL = Real Life.)

Answers
First text – photo B   Second text – photo A

3. Discuss some of the issues raised in the texts with your students. For example, do they think virtual worlds are a good form of escapism? Is *Second Life* a good place to do business or to learn a language?
4. Now give each pair or group Part 3 and ask them to invent a description of the real-life person for their favourite avatar. Encourage students to use their imaginations. Then ask several groups to share their ideas with the class.
5. Finally, ask all students to design an avatar for themselves. They should justify their choices and link them to their personality. For example: *I've got butterfly wings because I'd love to be able to fly!*
6. Put students into groups and ask each person to describe their avatar to the rest of their group. Then ask some of the students to tell the whole class about the avatar they liked most in their group.

Follow-up

- Students write an essay about the advantages and disadvantages of virtual worlds and what they think the future holds regarding virtual worlds. Possible advantages may include: relaxing, fun way to meet new people, cheap way to have fun. Possible disadvantages may include: addictive, waste of time, unhealthy – spending time indoors on the computer, etc.
- Have a class debate. Half the class think virtual worlds should be banned and the other half are in favour of them. Give students time to think of their arguments and then hold a debate or let students discuss it in groups.

2.3 Virtual worlds

Part 1

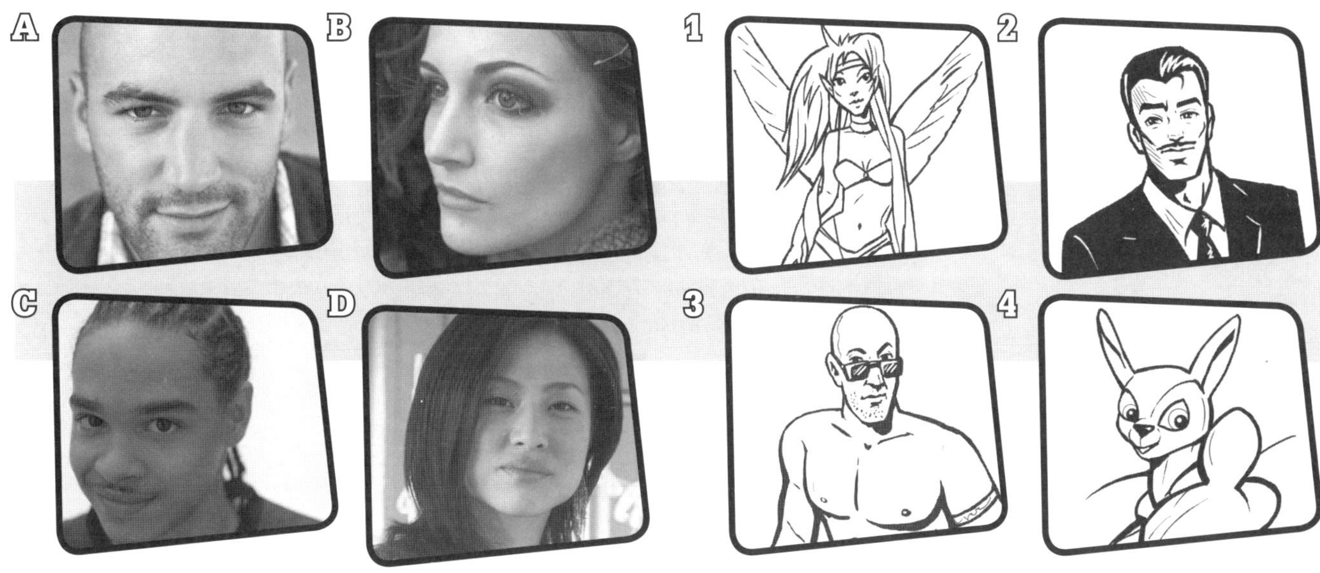

A
B
1
2
C
D
3
4

Part 2

I work in a designer clothes shop in my real life. After a long day on my feet there's nothing more relaxing than going into *Second Life*. It's pure escapism for me. When I created my avatar, I created a fantasy character, who looked nothing like me. I almost chose a male avatar but in the end decided on this one. I spend a lot of time making her look beautiful. I'm going to a fancy dress party this weekend and I'm going to dress as my avatar. Some people may find that weird, to overlap 'real life' and 'Second Life', but I think it's natural!

In real life I'm the editor of a technology magazine called *Techie News* and now I carry out a lot of business in *Second Life*. I created my avatar to look like me so that when I meet clients both in SL and RL they can recognise me. Although I like to think that I'm slightly better-looking! *Second Life* has opened up so many opportunities for our business. *Techie News* has built its own island there and it's now our main platform for advertising. Apart from working in *Second Life*, I'm also studying. I'm learning Japanese in a school there too!

Part 3

Musical postcards

Language focus
past simple

Key vocabulary
types of music, feelings and holidays (specific vocabulary will depend on how students react to the music)

Skills focus
writing a postcard; reading: skimming for general meaning

Level
elementary

Time
45 minutes

Preparation
one photocopy for each student; coloured pens or pencils if possible; a recording of a song or piece of music
Reggae and samba tend to produce beach scenes, and dance or techno music – cityscapes or futuristic scenes. These are probably the best choices for lower-level students. Classical or new age music usually produce more abstract designs which may be more appropriate for higher-level students to talk about.

Extra notes
This activity can be used with all ages and levels as the language is generated by the students themselves.

Warm-up

1. Ask students to write down the answers to these questions.
   1 What's your favourite song at the moment?
   2 What type of music makes you feel happy?
   3 Is there any type of music, or songs, that makes you feel sad?
   4 How many hours a day do you spend listening to music?
   5 How important is music to you?
2. Students compare answers with a partner or feed back to the class.

Main activity

1. Choose a piece of music that you think your students will enjoy (see Preparation).
2. If possible students should sit in a circle. Give each student a copy of the activity sheet and ask them to fold it in half so they only focus on the top rectangle.
3. Tell students to listen to the music and draw whatever comes into their minds in the rectangle. As long as music plays the students should keep drawing. Encourage them to use colour too.
4. After 20 seconds or so, stop the music. Students should stop drawing immediately and pass their activity sheet to the person next to them.
5. After six or seven changes, or when the song finishes, the students should keep the sheet they were drawing on most recently. Now each student has a picture in the top rectangle that is a combination of many students' artwork.
6. Ask a few volunteers to show their pictures to the class and describe them, or put students into pairs to describe their pictures to each other.
7. Tell students to unfold their activity sheets and ask them to imagine that the top picture is the front of a postcard. The section below is the back of the postcard. Ask students to imagine they are on holiday in the place depicted in the drawing and to write a postcard to a friend describing what they did during their holiday. For example:
   Hi Mateu!
   I'm in the Caribbean! It's hot and sunny and there are lots of palm trees. Yesterday I went to this fantastic beach. I swam in the sea and in the evening I danced with a handsome man. I think you can see him in the picture!
   See you soon,
   Isabel.
8. Cut the postcards and the pictures in half and spread them all out on a table, or stick them around the wall. Ask students to look at all the pictures and to match them to the texts.

Follow-up

- Each student should take their written postcard and their picture and stick them together with a piece of card in the middle to make a display. Younger students may enjoy making a mobile to hang their cards from.
- Instead of writing postcards, students imagine that the pictures are photographs they took themselves. They should explain where they were and what they were doing when they took the photo.

3.1 Musical postcards

fold here

Music fans

Language focus
question forms;
people + plural verb
(*people* ***have*** *not* ***has***)

Key vocabulary
concert, download, instrument, lyrics, musical taste, singer, types of music

Skills focus
speaking: asking questions; writing: summarising information

Level
intermediate

Time
50 minutes

Preparation
one photocopy for each student

Extra notes
This activity will give you an insight into the music tastes of your students. You can incorporate music they like, or information about singers that interest them, into future classes.

Warm-up

- Have a song playing as your students enter the classroom. Make it a song that is popular with them and ask them some general questions about the song and the singer or group. Ask students how long they spend listening to music each day and how important music is in their lives.

Main activity

1. Give each student a copy of the activity sheet.
2. If your students are familiar with 'Find someone who …' mingle activities this task will need little explanation. However, rather than simply finding one person in the room who fulfils the statements, they should find three people who fulfil them, and also find out as much extra information as possible.
3. If this type of task is new to your students, demonstrate a few of the questions. Ask students to look at the top two rows of the chart and to tell you the questions they will need to ask: *Have you been to a concert recently?* and *What type of music do you like?* If necessary, write the questions on the board for the weaker students to refer to during the activity.
4. Ask several students *Have you been to a concert recently?* until someone says *Yes.* Write their name in the Name column. Then ask a follow-up question like *Who did you see?* and write this information in the Extra information column.
5. Ask your students to complete the two blank rows with some information they'd really like to find out from their classmates to personalise the task. Tell students they don't have to ask the questions in order and they don't have to ask each person *all* the questions; they can pick and choose as they go along.
6. Before students begin the task, ensure everyone is standing up and can mingle freely with one another. They should all have a notebook to lean on to make writing their answers easier.
7. Set a time limit for the group mingle. When the first student has finished, stop the activity.
8. Now, using the information they have gathered from their classmates, they should complete the box at the bottom with a brief summary of their findings. For example: *Enrique and Alba have been to a concert recently. They both saw Lily Allen at the sports stadium last month. I also found out that only one student, Pau, can play an instrument. He plays the drums.*
9. Ask a few students to read their summary to the class.

Follow-up

- Ask students who are the most popular groups or singers amongst the class. Draw up a list of the class top five. If any of the artists sing in English, ask the class which are their favourite songs by these artists. Make a note of them and prepare some song activities for future classes.
- Students think of how to finish the statement 'Music is …'. They can write whatever they want and, if you have time, decorate the statement with pictures of their favourite groups.

3.2 Music fans

Find classmates who …	Name	Name	Name	Extra information
… have been to a concert recently.				
… like the same type of music as you.				
… have very different musical tastes from you.				
… listen to music whenever they can.				
… can play a musical instrument.				
… download music from the Internet.				
… would like to be musicians or singers.				
… know the lyrics to a whole song in English.				
…				
…				

I found out that

Music festival

Language focus
offering suggestions and expressing opinions

Key vocabulary
language to talk about music festivals: *advertising, band, camping facilities, group, security, site, stage, stalls*

Skills focus
speaking: group planning, discussing and presenting ideas

Level
upper-intermediate

Time
60 minutes

Preparation
one photocopy for each group of 2 or 3 students

Extra notes
This could be extended into a mini project by students going into great detail about all the planning elements of the festival.

Warm-up

1. Ask your students to write three questions about music festivals. For example: *Have you ever been to a music festival? Would you like to go to a music festival?*
2. Put students into pairs or small groups to ask one another their questions. Ask the class for some feedback on what they found out.

Main activity

1. Put students into pairs or small groups and tell them they are going to plan a music festival to be held in or near their town in the near future.
2. Give each group a copy of the activity sheet. Ask students to look at it and to describe what they can see in the four photos.
3. In their groups students should consider all the aspects that are shown in the photos and make notes on the activity sheet when they make their decisions. Students may have to encourage and persuade the other group members to agree with their preferences. If your students need more assistance and prompts for what to discuss, use the following questions to help them.
   What type of music festival is it?
   Which groups or singers will play at the festival?
   Where will it take place?
   How will you go about getting permission to use the site?
   How long will it last?
   How many people will be able to go to the music festival?
   Will people be able to camp on the site? Should you also offer more comfortable accommodation?
   How much will a ticket cost? (Remember, if you have very famous groups and singers they will need to be paid a lot!)
   What jobs will you need to advertise – security guards, ticket inspectors, first aid teams, etc?
   What will be special about your festival? Why will people want to come?
   How will you advertise the festival?
4. When the groups have a clear idea about the type of festival they would like to see in their town, ask each group to present their music festival to the class. Hold a class vote to decide which group presented the best ideas for the music festival.

Follow-up

- Students write a radio advertisement for the music festival they have planned.
- Ask students to find out about some other festivals they are interested in, not just music festivals. Use a search engine to find out about them. The Edinburgh Festival, the Isle of Wight Festival, the Reading Festival and T in the Park are just some of the UK festivals they could research. They could also research festivals in their own country.

3.3 Music festival

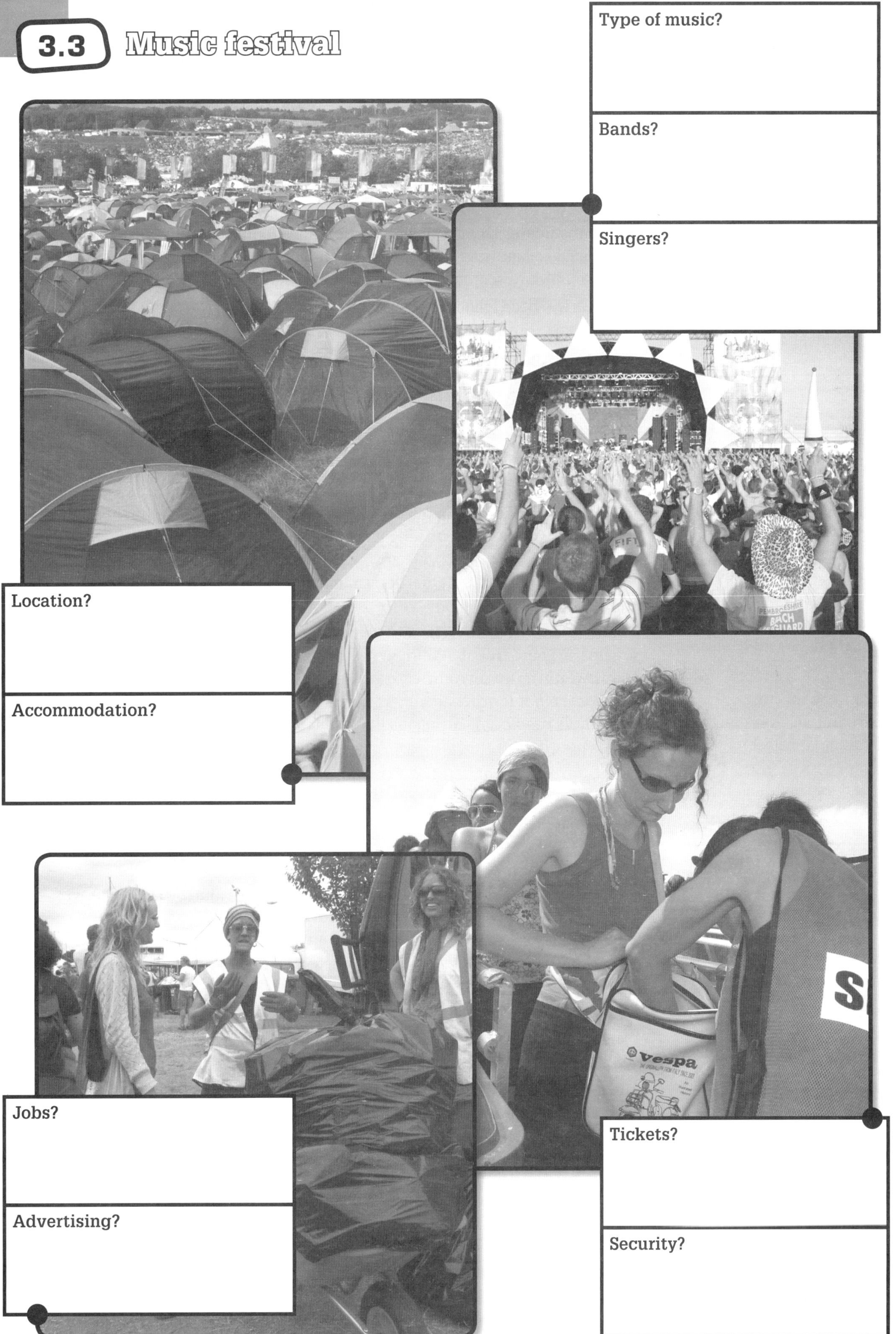

Type of music?
Bands?
Singers?
Location?
Accommodation?
Jobs?
Advertising?
Tickets?
Security?

Workbusters

Language focus
relative pronouns, jobs, prices

Key vocabulary
jobs and prices

Skills focus
speaking: pronunciation of prices, answering questions

Level
elementary

Time
45 minutes

Preparation
one photocopy for the class, enlarged and displayed where everyone can see it

Extra notes
The game is useful to expand on the basic lexical set of jobs usually introduced in low-level course books.

Warm-up

1. Revise the job vocabulary that students will need for the game, using any of your usual vocabulary recycling techniques: flash cards, playing Hangman, doing a job word search, playing a job guessing game, an A–Z of jobs, etc.
2. Draw on the board the three currency symbols used on the game board: pounds (£), dollars ($) and euros (€). Ask students where these currencies are used, and if you have any coins or notes in these currencies, bring them in to class.
3. Ask students what they have bought recently and how much the items cost. Write the costs on the board in words and figures and ask the whole class to read them out aloud to practise pronunciation.

Main activity

1. Display a copy of the game board so that everyone can see it – either by enlarging it onto A3 and sticking it on the board, or copy and project it onto the board. If you have a data projector, scan the board into the computer to project it. You keep a copy of the Questions and answers (or appoint a student to act as quizmaster).
2. Students work in teams. The aim of the game is for each team to complete a line across the board from left to right or from top to bottom (including diagonally). By answering questions correctly, the hexagons are won and coloured in (a different colour for each team). The other team can try to block the progress of their rivals by winning hexagons that interrupt their path.
3. To ask for a specific hexagon, the team must say, for example: *We want four euros, thirty-five cents, please.* If you are expecting correct pronunciation, insist on it in order for the team to get the question. Then you (or a student who is acting as quizmaster) should read out the corresponding question. Set a time limit for teams to answer in, in order to keep the game snappy.
4. If the team answers correctly and within the time limit, colour in the hexagon with their colour, or use their team symbol. Then pass the turn to the other team. If the team gets an answer wrong or takes too long to answer, the other team can have a go at answering. If they are right, they win the hexagon.
5. If your students are competitive, assign an accountant who can make a note of how much money each team wins as they play. The team wins the amount on the hexagons they win.
6. Continue the game until one team manages to get across the board from left to right or from top to bottom. They are the winners.
7. You could also then add up how much each team has won, and see who has won the most money. The accountant would have to look up the exchange rates and convert the pounds, dollars and euros to their own currency. Exchange rates are easily found on the Internet.

Follow-up

- Ask the students to write several questions each. The questions could be related to another area of vocabulary you'd like to revise. Put all the questions together and play the game again in a future class.
- Students think about their top three and worst three jobs and write a list of advantages and disadvantages of each.

4.1 Workbusters

£14.99
€5.50
€4.35
$1.98
£9.19
$2.47
$3.33
£12.18
£11.76
€6.25
€9.45
€8.80
€13.30
$3.50
£14.59
£7.13
£11.45
$2.75
$18.87
$12.50
£19.74
€15.99
£3.45
€17.60
£1.19

Questions and answers

	Question	Answer
€4.35	**Q:** Name 3 jobs where you work with the general public.	**A:** e.g. shop assistant, police officer, bank clerk, doctor
£12.18	**Q:** If you earn 7 pounds an hour and work for 20 hours per week, how much do you earn in 2 weeks?	**A:** 280 pounds
€13.30	**Q:** Name 5 jobs where you have to wear a uniform.	**A:** e.g. doctor, nurse, police officer, traffic warden, soldier
$2.75	**Q:** Name 3 jobs that, in your opinion, pay too much money.	**A:** students' own answer
£3.45	**Q:** Name 3 jobs that, in your opinion, pay too little money.	**A:** students' own answer
£14.99	**Q:** What's the name of a person who cuts hair?	**A:** hairdresser (barber for men)
$2.47	**Q:** What's the name of a doctor for animals?	**A:** vet
€9.45	**Q:** Name 3 jobs that begin with the letter T.	**A:** e.g. teacher, trainer, technician, tourist guide
£7.13	**Q:** Name 2 jobs where you must know at least 2 languages.	**A:** e.g. translator, interpreter, tourist guide
£19.74	**Q:** What's the name of a person who sells meat?	**A:** butcher
$1.98	**Q:** What's the name of a person who makes bread?	**A:** baker
£11.76	**Q:** If you work for 8 hours a day, 3 days a week and earn $7 per hour, how much do you earn in a week?	**A:** $168
$3.50	**Q:** Name three jobs that begin with the letter D.	**A:** e.g. dentist, designer, dancer, driver, diver
$18.87	**Q:** What's the name of a person who works in a shop?	**A:** shop assistant
€17.60	**Q:** Name 2 people who work in a restaurant.	**A:** e.g. chef, cook, waiter, waitress, cleaner, manager
€5.50	**Q:** Name 3 jobs which people do outside.	**A:** e.g. gardener, builder, refuse collector, flower seller
$3.33	**Q:** What's the name of a person who designs buildings?	**A:** architect
€8.80	**Q:** If you work from 9 o'clock until 6.30 and have a 1-hour break for lunch, how many hours do you actually work?	**A:** 8 and a half hours
£11.45	**Q:** Name a job where you make things out of wood	**A:** carpenter, joiner, sculptor
€15.99	**Q:** Name a job where you write articles for a newspaper.	**A:** journalist
£9.19	**Q:** Name 3 jobs where you have to travel a lot.	**A:** e.g. pilot, lorry driver, flight attendant, businessperson
€6.25	**Q:** Name 3 jobs where you usually have to wear a hat.	**A:** e.g. police officer, traffic warden, baker, builder, soldier
£14.59	**Q:** Name 3 jobs that begin with the letter A.	**A:** e.g. architect, artist, archaeologist, actor
$12.50	**Q:** EARTECH is an anagram. What's the job?	**A:** teacher
£1.19	**Q:** TALROOFLEB is an anagram. What's the job?	**A:** footballer

Holiday jobs

Language focus
modal verbs: *must, should, might*, etc., questions forms

Key vocabulary
jobs and interviews: *babysitter, call centre, CV, efficient, experience, holiday/part-time job, interview, job centre, residence for the elderly, responsible, shop assistant, telephone manner, waiter, waitress, warehouse*

Skills focus
speaking: asking and answering questions

Level
intermediate

Time
50 minutes

Preparation
one photocopy, cut up, for each student

Warm-up

1. If where you're teaching it's common for teenagers to have part-time jobs in the holidays or at weekends, start by asking students about the types of job they've done, whether or not they enjoyed them, etc. Direct the conversation towards the process of getting the job and talk about job interviews.
2. If your students have yet to experience having part-time jobs, you need to get them into the mindset of thinking about looking for and applying for a part-time job. Brainstorm ideas on the sorts of job they think they'd enjoy doing and talk about the advantages and disadvantages of having part-time jobs.

Main activity

1. Set the scene for the students and create an incentive for them to want to get a part-time job. For example, they're saving up money for an end-of-year school trip abroad or they want to buy the latest technological gadget. When you have set the scene, ask students how they're going to find a part-time job. Listen to their suggestions and if nobody has already suggested it, explain the idea of a job centre or a 'temping agency' that helps people find temporary work.
2. Give out the activity sheets and ask students to look at the job adverts in pairs or small groups. Ask them which jobs they think may be the most interesting.
3. Look together at the Interviewer check list. The list just has points to guide the interviewers – they will still need to formulate their own questions.
4. Divide the class in half. One group will take the role of the job seekers, the other group will be the interviewers at the job centre.
5. Give students time to prepare for the interviews. The job seekers should choose the job they prefer and then try to predict the questions they'll be asked. The interviewers should now write some questions they will ask the job seekers. They need to be prepared to ask questions about each of the jobs so they may want to write a specific question for each job.
6. Now, pair a job seeker with an interviewer to carry out the interview. Monitor the students carefully as they do the role play.
7. When they have finished, ask the interviewers whether they would give the job seeker the job or not.
8. If time permits, rotate the job seekers and let them have another interview with a different interviewer.
9. Now change roles so the job seekers become the interviewers and vice versa.

Follow-up

- Set up part of the classroom as the office and hold group interviews with two or three interviewers and several job seekers at a time. Students who are not in the role play could vote on who was the best interviewer and who they would give the job to. If you have the equipment, you could film the interviews. As you watch them back, you could analyse the body language of the job seekers and discuss what you think is the best way to behave in a stressful interview situation.
- Students compile a list of tips for passing interviews. Before they make their lists, discuss dress code, body language, behaviour, researching the job, etc.

4.2 Holiday jobs

Babysitter

Young person required to look after three children during the summer holidays (8.30am–6pm Mon–Fri).
Applicants should be:

- very responsible
- caring
- imaginative and energetic and have experience of babysitting

Waiter / waitress

A busy and vibrant café in the town centre is looking for two part-time waiters for the summer holidays.

Six hours per day, four days per week (including some weekends).
Applicants should be friendly and efficient.
Previous experience as a waiter isn't necessary.

Shop assistant

Super Sports is looking for two part-time shop assistants to join their dynamic team. If you love sports and are fit and healthy-looking you may be just who they are looking for. No previous experience necessary, as they will send you on a *Super Sports* training day to teach you all you need to know.

Carer for the elderly

Are you kind, caring and extremely patient? Do you like meeting new, interesting people?

A local home for the elderly is looking for five young people to work in their modern residence. Duties include day-to-day care of the residents, help at meal times and organising activities like bingo or quizzes.

Flexible hours and all meals included.

No experience necessary.

Call centre

Speedy Net Connection

is looking for a team of tele-operators for their new call centre. They need enthusiastic young people who are polite and are interested in working in the area of sales.

If you like working independently, have some experience in sales and have a good telephone manner, this could be the job for you.

Good pay with bonuses for sales.

MOBILE PHONE WAREHOUSE

GREEN mobile phone warehouse is looking for responsible warehouse staff to check and pack the latest technology mobile phones.

Attractive pay with a free mobile phone included!
Part-time, holiday work and permanent jobs available.

No experience necessary.

Interviewer check list
✔ Is the interviewee responsible? Ask about previous jobs, punctuality and reliability.
✔ Is the interviewee enthusiastic? Do they show an interest in the job? Do they ask questions?
✔ Does the interviewee have any experience? Has the interviewee got the skills needed for the job?
✔ Overall impression? Was the interviewee well prepared? Will the employer be happy if I recommend them?

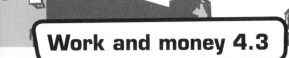

Are you money mad?

Language focus
expressing opinions, money vocabulary

Key vocabulary
bill, cash machine, charity, cheque, credit card, earn, purse, salary, to spend, to win, wallet

Skills focus
reading: answering questions
speaking: discussing

Level
upper-intermediate

Time
35 minutes

Preparation
one photocopy for each pair of students or for each group of 4 or 5 students (see step 2)

Warm-up

1. One way to begin the class is with a guided visualisation. Say:
   I want you to imagine it's the year ________ (put a year when your students will be about 30). You are in your thirties. It's a normal Monday morning and you wake up. What's your bedroom like? You have a shower and have breakfast. You leave your house and go to work. Have a look back at your house before you leave. What's your house like? Is it big, is it small? You travel to work. How do you get there? You arrive at your place of work. Where is it? What do you do all day? Do you earn a lot of money in your job? How do you feel at the end of the day?
2. When you have finished, say to your students *OK, sit up and draw or make notes about the images you saw as I was speaking to you.* Give students two minutes to gather their thoughts. Some students find it a lot easier than others to visualise images.
3. Put students into pairs and ask them to explain what they saw to each other. Then gather some feedback from the whole class. In order for them to reflect on the possible significance of money in their future, ask some questions such as:
   Was your house luxurious? *Were you doing a well paid job?*
   Did you see yourself in a powerful position at work? *How did you travel to work?*

Main activity

1. Give out the activity sheets and tell students they are going to do a quiz to find out how important money is in their lives.
2. Put students into pairs to work through the quiz, as if they were looking through a magazine together. Ensure they fold over the Score section so they're not tempted to look. You could always cut off this part of the activity sheet if you don't trust them! If you prefer, put students into groups of four or five with just one copy of the quiz each and ask one student to be in charge of asking the questions and noting everyone's answers.
3. When they have finished, they should add up their points.
4. Now put two pairs together to compare their answers.
5. Ask the class for some feedback on the quiz results.

Follow-up

- Ask students to look back at question 3 of the quiz and to write three more dilemma questions in their pairs. Then put two pairs together to swap their questions and answer each other's dilemmas.
- Use the following sayings to extend discussion on the importance of money and work. Write up the sayings on the board. Put students into small groups and tell them to discuss each saying for two to three minutes. Tell them when it is time to move on to the next saying. Monitor carefully and encourage the students to express their opinions clearly and coherently.
  Look after the pennies and the pounds will look after themselves.
  Money attracts money.
  Work hard and play hard.
  Work to live, not live to work.
  You should always save some money for a rainy day.

4.3 Are you money mad?

Are you money mad?

Try our quiz to find out how important money and work are to you.

1 To what extent do you agree with the following sayings?

A Money makes the world go round.
- a Totally agree
- b Neither agree nor disagree
- c Totally disagree.

B If you've got it … spend it!
- a Totally agree
- b Neither agree nor disagree
- c Totally disagree.

C Work to live, not live to work.
- a Totally agree
- b Neither agree nor disagree
- c Totally disagree.

D Money brings happiness.
- a Totally agree
- b Neither agree nor disagree
- c Totally disagree.

2 Rank the following things in order of importance. Put the most important first.

family friends happiness home love money work

3 What would you do in these situations?

A You win $1,000,000 in the lottery. Would you …
- a give a large part of it to friends, family and to charity?
- b not tell a soul and keep it all? Nowadays a million isn't so much.
- c spend it all?!

B You are offered a job you hate but it pays a huge salary. Would you …
- a take the job. The salary is irresistible!
- b decline the job. You would prefer to do something you enjoy.
- c do the job for just long enough to save a lot of money.

C You have lots of free time in the holidays. Would you …
- a do some voluntary work?
- b find a job to earn some money?
- c enjoy yourself?

4 What are these money-related objects called?

a 

d 
The Ivy

e 

b 

c 

f 
CASH

fold here

Score

1
- A a 10 b 5 c 0
- B a 0 b 5 c 10
- C a 0 b 5 c 10
- D a 10 b 5 c 0

2 If money is first or second place – 10 points
If money is in third, fourth or fifth place – 5 points
If money is in sixth or seventh place – 0 points

3
- A a 0 b 10 c 5
- B a 10 b 0 c 5
- C a 0 b 10 c 5

4 Five points for each correct answer.
- a a wallet
- b a purse
- c a cheque
- d a bill
- e a credit card
- f a cash machine

Total points

0–40	45–75	80–110
You're really not very interested in money. It's not top of your list of priorities.	You're not obsessed with money, but you realise it can sometimes be very important.	You are money mad! Try not to let money rule your life though!

Funny comic strips

Language focus
present simple and present continuous to tell simple stories

Key vocabulary
comedy, comic, funny, to laugh, to make someone laugh

Skills focus
speaking and writing: storytelling

Level
elementary

Time
50 minutes

Preparation
one photocopy, cut up, for each pair of students

Warm-up

1. Stick some pictures of comedians or actors on the board and ask your students to rank them from the funniest to the least funny.
2. Ask your students *When was the last time you really laughed a lot?* Students could work in pairs, and then you can ask some of the students to tell the whole class about their partner's recent funny moment.

Main activity

1. Put students into pairs and give each pair one of the two comic strips with the final frame cut off.
2. Ask them to look at the pictures carefully and to think about how they would describe the events in the comic strip. Tell them that the last frame is missing and ask them to imagine how the comic strip ends. Give each pair ten to fifteen minutes to add the dialogue to the speech bubbles, think of the ending and practise describing the events.
3. If you think your students are going to struggle to think of a dialogue for the speech bubbles in the comic strips you could put the suggested answers (below) on the board in a jumbled order for students to choose from.

Suggested answers
Comic strip 1: Oh no, not again! / See you tomorrow! / I believe I said half past eleven! / Oh Mum, can we talk about this please?

Comic strip 2: Dad, can I stay 1hr + please? We r having fun.* / OK. But you must be back by half past ten. / I'll teach you how to send text messages again if you like. / I like my system better! (* Texting language: hr = hour; + = more; r = are)

4. Now, put two pairs together to make groups of four, ensuring that the pairs you join both had *different* comic strips. Pairs take it in turns to describe their comic strip to the other pair and to explain their ending.
5. Now give the students the final frame of each comic strip so they can compare the endings with their own. Ask the class for feedback about how similar or different their endings were and if they found the comic strips funny or not.

Follow-up

- Ask students what other topics, of interest to teenagers, may be good for creating funny comic strips. Have they ever been in any funny situations with their own parents that would make funny comic strips? They could make their own comic strip about a situation they've been in, or an invented scenario.
- Carry out a class survey about humour. Use questions such as *Who's your favourite comedian? What's your favourite joke? What's your favourite sitcom?*
- Have a joke-telling competition in the class. All students should think of their favourite joke, translate it into English with your help and the aid of a dictionary, and tell it to the class. Beware that some jokes, especially those containing puns, don't easily translate into a different language! You could judge the competition on the basis of a 'Laughometer', where the winner is the one who gets the longest or loudest laugh from the class.

5.1 Funny comic strips

BEEP! - BEEP! - BEEP!

Bad jokes

Language focus
questions and answers

Key vocabulary
telling jokes: *to laugh, to tell a joke*

Skills focus
reading: matching
speaking: telling jokes

Level
intermediate

Time
40 minutes

Preparation
one photocopy, cut up, for each group of 3 or 4 students

Warm-up

1. Ask students to tell their partners what makes them laugh. Write their ideas on the board in a mind map. Elicit funny television programmes, comedians, funny friends, films, cartoons, etc.
2. Now ask students what's the funniest thing they've seen or heard recently. Give them a minute or so thinking time. Some students may tell a short story or a joke. Translating jokes into another language is often really difficult, so you may have to help.

Main activity

1. Give one cut-up activity sheet to each group of three or four students.
2. Students should first of all try to match the two parts of each joke. Warn them that the jokes are really rather bad and it may be difficult for them to understand them all at first. You may have to offer support to help them get the jokes. Encourage students to use a process of elimination and to look for clues in the language – for example some of the colours mentioned in the jokes give big clues.
3. When they have matched them, ask the groups to rank them from the funniest to the least funny.
4. Compare the rankings between the groups.
5. Then talk to students about the way jokes are told, as it's often *the way* they are told that makes them funny. Give some examples by telling a few of the jokes (or others of your own) to the class in an exaggerated way.
6. Ask students to choose their favourite joke and to practise telling it in their groups, e.g.

   Student A: *Why did the tomato turn red?*
   Student B: *I don't know. Why did the tomato turn red?*
   Student A: *Because it saw the salad dressing.*
7. If you have some outgoing students, ask for a few volunteers to tell their jokes to the class.
8. Ask students to think of some of their favourite jokes and, in their groups, with your help and the help of a dictionary, translate them into English. Each group should think of four or five jokes and write them out in strips like in the activity they've just done. They could be 'question and answer' jokes, or they could be in a different style, but presented in two parts.
9. Now swap the jokes the students have written between the groups and ask them to match up the two halves of each joke.

Follow-up

- Students produce a wall display, or a class joke book, of the jokes they've written to put in the corridor or classroom.
- Ask students to bring in something that makes them laugh for the next class. It may be a photo or object that reminds them of a funny incident, a book, a comic, a picture of a comedian or comic actor, a joke, etc. Put students into groups to talk about their items. Then ask each group to feed back to the class.

5.2 Bad jokes

Why did the tomato turn red?	Because it saw the salad dressing.
What does the little computer call its Dad?	Data.
What runs but never walks?	Water.
Waiter, your thumb's in my soup!	Don't worry, madam, it's not too hot.
What's white on the outside, green on the inside and jumps?	A frog sandwich.
What do sea monsters eat?	Fish and ships.
What's small and green and goes up and down?	An olive in a lift.
What animal is grey, has four legs, a long nose and is very big?	A giant, long-nosed mouse.
What's black and white and read all over?	A newspaper.
What has eighty-eight keys but can't open any doors?	A piano.

Watch out! There's a joke about!

Language focus
present tenses for story telling

Key vocabulary
gag, to make someone laugh, to play a joke on someone, practical joke, sense of humour bar code, goat, gorilla, piercing, snooker, stand (noun), tongue, weighted

Skills focus
reading and speaking: ranking
writing: practical jokes

Level
upper-intermediate

Time
50 minutes

Preparation
one photocopy, cut up, for each group of 4 students

Warm-up

- Put students into pairs and tell them to ask one another the following questions.
  When was the last time you laughed so much you cried?
  Who's your favourite comedian?
  What's the funniest film or TV programme you've ever seen?
  Who's the funniest member of your family?
  Are you good at telling jokes?
  Have you ever played a practical joke on somebody?

Main activity

1. Ask the class if they know any television programmes that are based on playing practical jokes on members of the public. If your country has such a programme, showing a recording of a few practical jokes in action would set the scene nicely. If this type of programme isn't shown where you're teaching, give the students an idea of the type of programme that the practical jokes they are going to read about are based on. It's possible to see them on the Internet. If you type 'Just for laughs' into a search engine you can watch a huge selection of practical jokes from a Canadian television programme.
2. Tell students to imagine they're working on the production team of a TV programme called *Watch Out! There´s a Joker About!* They have to decide which are the funniest pranks.
3. Put students into 'production teams' of four and give each team a set of practical joke cards. Students should take two each.
4. Each student should read their cards, then explain their practical jokes to the team from memory, without looking back at their cards.
5. When the team have heard a selection of practical jokes, they should rank them from the funniest to the least funny. All members of the team should make a note of their top three jokes.
6. Then pair students with members of different production teams to compare how similar or different their choices for their three favourite jokes were.
7. Now put them back into their original teams, and tell them that the production team has been asked to think of new practical jokes for the next series of the programme. Each team needs to think of a joke and write down their ideas.
8. If time permits, each team could perform their practical joke for the whole class to see. Then the class can vote on their favourite joke.

Follow-up

- If your students do perform their practical jokes, you could film them with a hidden 'fly-on-the-wall' camera and make your own TV programme. This could be used to show to other classes you have as a basis for a similar lesson.
- Students write a review of the new series of *Watch Out! There´s a Joker About!* for a magazine or newspaper.
- In pairs, one student imagines they were the victim of one of the many practical jokes mentioned in the lesson. The other student is their best friend. Students work together to write the dialogue between the friends, just after one of them has been tricked.

5.3 Watch out! There's a joker about!

Bin man!

Location: A busy street in a residential area

Joke: One of the local residents brings out their bag of rubbish to throw into the rubbish bin. Little do they know that there's a man dressed as a monster (an actor) waiting for them inside the bin. As they put the rubbish bag into the bin, he pops out and gives them a fright. Ha-ha!

New drink tasting

Location: A busy shopping centre

Joke: A company promoting a new soft drink offers their new product to the shoppers to try. The stand is very attractive, with pictures of fruit, and it appears to be the launch of a new, delicious drink. Many shoppers want to try it on a warm day. However, the drink is in fact coloured water with lots of salt in, so tastes absolutely disgusting. Ha-ha!

The postman knocks

Location: A residential area

Joke: A postman knocks on the door of an unsuspecting victim and asks them to sign for a package that he has in his van for them. Once they've signed the form he goes to the van and gets out a goat and gives it to them. Ha-ha!

Snooker ball

Location: A games hall

Joke: A man goes into a games hall full of people playing snooker. He swaps the white ball for one he has in his pocket when the players aren't looking. The ball he has is weighted strangely so when the players hit it, the ball goes in a circle rather than in a straight line. The players are very puzzled. Ha-ha!

Gorilla cage

Location: A zoo

Joke: At the zoo, the zoo keeper asks an unsuspecting visitor to help him take a bag of food into an empty gorilla's cage. They help him and go into the cage. Then a man in a gorilla suit comes into the cage. The zoo keeper tells the helper to keep calm and they spend a few minutes trying to get out of the cage, before the victim realises the gorilla is in fact an actor dressed up in a very convincing gorilla costume! Ha-ha!

Magic tongue

Location: A supermarket

Joke: The cashier on the checkout in the supermarket has a piercing in her tongue. When a shopper comes to the checkout to pay, she uses her tongue to pass the barcodes of the groceries into the cash till, much to the surprise of the unsuspecting shopper! The cashier is, of course, an actress. Ha-ha!

Cream cake

Location: On the street

Joke: A lady walks along the street eating a cream cake. She sneezes and gets cream all over her face. She asks passers-by to help her clean her face with a tissue. While they are helping her she sneezes again and covers the helper with cream too. Of course the lady is an actress and the whole silly scenario is caught on film. Ha-ha!

Hot dog parking

Location: A shopping centre car park

Joke: There are lots of cars parked in the car park outside a busy shopping centre. While the owner of one of the cars is in the centre, the *Watch Out! There's a Joker about!* team puts a portable hot dog stall with wheels over the car. The car owner comes out, they can't find their car, and see a hot dog stall where their car was parked. Ha-ha!

Extreme makeover

Language focus
describing and comparing people's appearances
present simple, present continuous, clothes

Key vocabulary
He's wearing … , She's got … , He looks … bag, baggy, baseball cap, better, blouse, briefcase, cardigan, ear-rings, flat / high-heel shoes, glasses, haircut, laptop, make-up, rucksack, sandals, suit, tattoo, tight, tights, worse

Skills focus
speaking and writing: describing people, discussing

Level
elementary

Time
50 minutes

Preparation
one photocopy for each group of 4 students, cut up into 'before' and 'after' pictures; (optional) photographs from the Internet – see step 5

Warm-up

1. All students need a blank strip of paper. Ask them to choose somebody in the class and to write a short physical description of them. If necessary in your class, remind students that you always expect them to respect their classmates and in this activity you want nice descriptions of each other.
2. Redistribute the descriptions so nobody has the one they wrote themselves.
3. Now, ask students to read the description and to write the name of the person they think it describes on the paper.
4. Ask several students to read their descriptions and their guesses out loud to check. Students are revising simple language for clothes and describing people during this activity, which they will need for the main activity.

Main activity

1. Put students into groups of four. Give each group a set of the 'before' pictures. Ask each student to take one picture and to describe the person in as much detail as possible to the group. They should do this as if they are introducing their character to the others. For example: *This is Jasmine. She's wearing baggy tracksuit trousers and a big T-shirt. She's got long hair …* etc.
2. Then explain to the group that the four teenagers in the pictures take part in a television makeover programme to get a totally new look. Ask the students to imagine what the makeover team are going to do to them to change the way they look. Students should make predictions in their groups.
3. Give out the four 'after' pictures to the groups. Now, students need to look at the pictures and to comment on the changes. Ask some questions to give students ideas on the types of comment they can make apart from the physical changes. For example: *Isabel now looks more confident and happier* or *Sam looks stupid! I think he looked better before the makeover.*
4. Each student now uses their 'before' and 'after' pictures to write a paragraph describing the appearance of the person both before and after the makeover.
5. If you want to extend this lesson and focus on television makeover programmes, have a look on the Internet (type 'extreme makeover') to find photographs from these programmes, some of which even involve plastic surgery to transform participants' looks. With higher levels you could use these as a lead-in to talking about the pros and cons of plastic surgery.

Follow-up

- If you have time (this would be good for a summer course or end-of-term activity) and the necessary equipment, you could make your own class version of a makeover show. Students bring in clothes to change into and take photos of their 'before' and 'after' looks. They then write about the photos of themselves with their two different images. If you have a camera, and plenty of time, you could even film them and make the TV programme!
- Collect some photos from fashion magazines. Ask students to choose a model and to write a short description of them. Stick the photos up around the classroom and redistribute the descriptions so that nobody has their own. Ask students to try to match the descriptions to the photos.

6.1 Extreme makeover

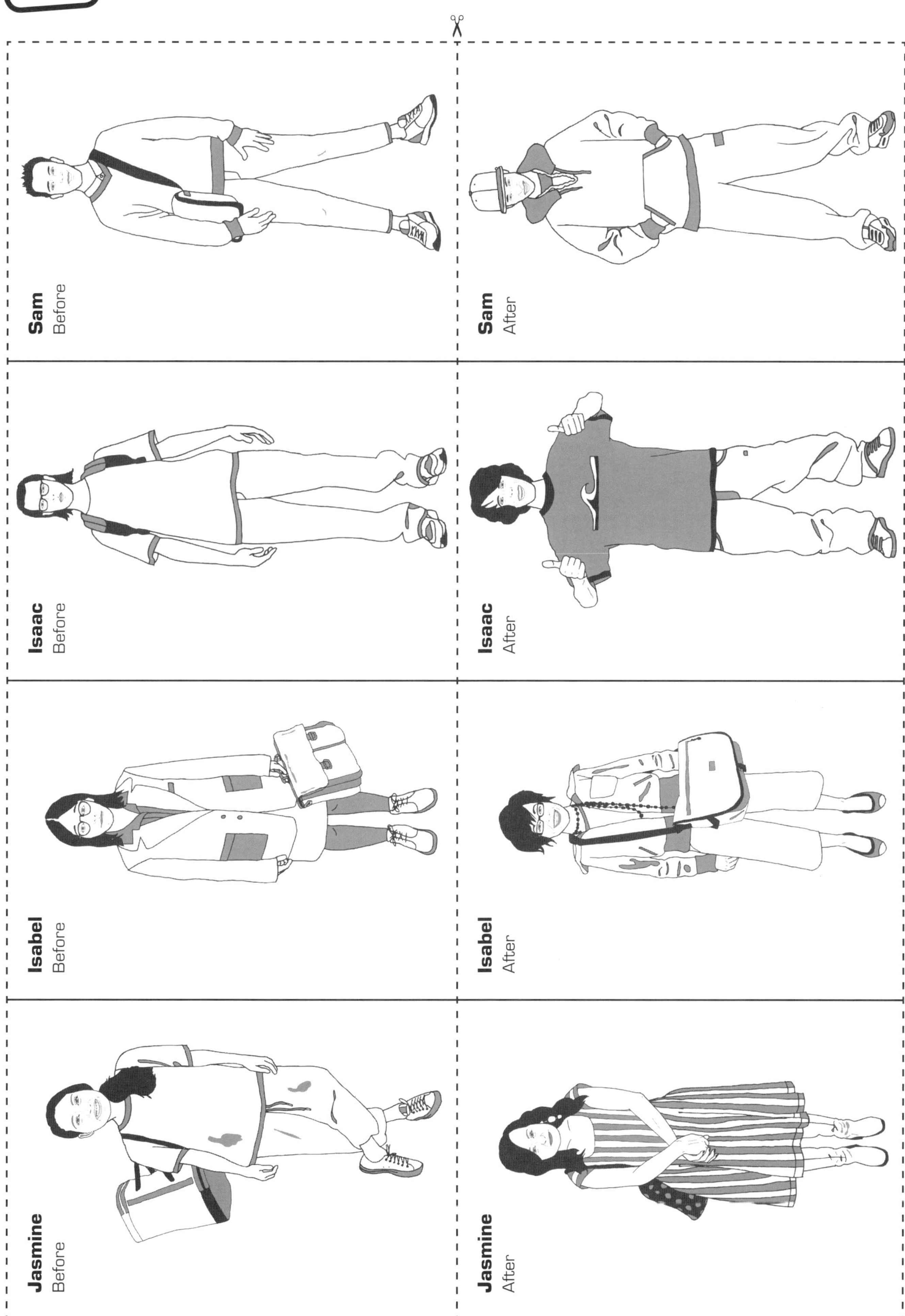

Sam
Before
Sam
After
Isaac
Before
Isaac
After
Isabel
Before
Isabel
After
Jasmine
Before
Jasmine
After

Teen tribes

Language focus
describing people and expressing opinions

Key vocabulary
clothes: *baggy, chino trousers, chunky, deck shoes, earphones, floppy hair, flowery, headscarf, hoody, polo shirt*
types of people: *goth, hippy, preppy, skater, techie, townie*

Skills focus
speaking: predicting, describing and discussing

Level
intermediate

Time
50 minutes

Preparation
one photocopy, cut up and clipped together, for each small group of students

Extra notes
Talking about teen tribes or groups could be a sensitive issue for some of your students who are uncomfortable with their own appearances.

Warm-up

1. Ask students to draw their favourite outfit, show it to a partner and ask each other questions about it. For example: *Where did you buy your favourite jeans? Is the T-shirt old or new?* You could start this activity by describing and drawing your favourite outfit on the board to give students an idea.
2. Ask a few students to tell the class about their partner's favourite outfit.

Main activity

1. Put students into small groups for this activity. Give each group a cut-up set of the word cards and tell them they refer to different 'teen tribes'. Ask each student in the group in turn to take a word card and to guess what type of people fit into that 'tribe'. Ask, for example, *What do these people do? What do they wear?* Some will be easier to guess than others, so keep this task short and snappy and if your students don't know, move on quickly to Step 2.
2. Now give out the pictures of the six people. Tell your students to try and match the people to the word cards. Ask if their predictions about the type of people were correct.
3. Now give out the description cards to each group and ask them to match them to the pictures and the word cards. When you have checked that each group has the right answers, ask the students what else they can tell you about these different groups.

Answers

Hippies 5 F	Townies 3 D	Goths 1 C
Skaters 2 E	Preppies 6 B	Technies 4 A

4. Ask students if there are similar or different types of 'teen tribes' in their country.
5. Now write several of the discussion statements below on the board. Set a time limit for students to discuss them in small groups.
   Appearance and 'looks' aren't important.
   Beauty is on the inside not the outside.
   Being an individual is more important than fitting into a 'group'.
   First impressions count.
   Your appearance shows your personality.

Follow-up

- Choose one of the discussion statements above and hold a class debate.
- Students make posters to show you what is 'in' and 'out' of fashion. Bring in some catalogues and magazines for them to cut up. Then they should write an explanation of the latest trends shown on the poster.
- Give each group one 'tribe' to write about. They could find pictures in magazines or on the Internet and write a description of the typical image of a member of that group.

6.2 Teen Tribes

Word cards

HIPPIES	TOWNIES	GOTHS
SKATERS	PREPPIES	TECHIES

Picture cards

1

2

3

4

I ♥ THE
MONSTER

5
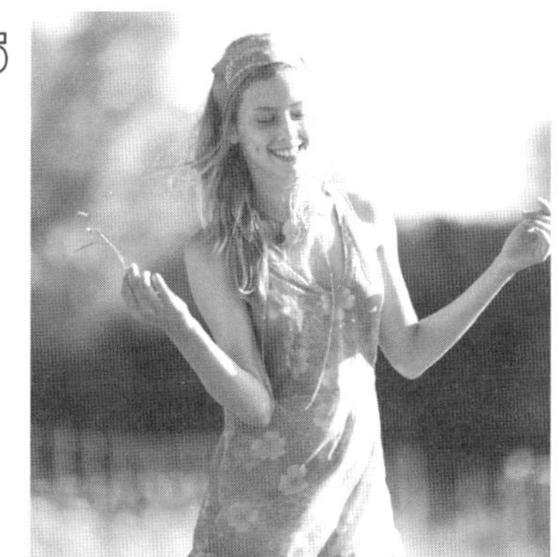

6

Description cards

A	B	C	D	E	F
The latest mobile phone Laptop Earphones	Floppy hair Chino trousers Bag Expensive jumper	Black clothes Pale skin Listen to heavy metal music	Hoodies Tracksuits Gold jewellery	Low, baggy trousers Baggy T-shirts Chunky trainers	Long skirts Flowery or patterned clothes Head scarves

Inside-out or not at all?

Language focus
questions, second conditional

Key vocabulary
acceptable, first date, first impression, piercing, plastic surgery, skin deep, tattoo

Skills focus
reading: questionnaire; speaking: asking and answering questions and comparing answers, discussing

Level
upper-intermediate

Time
50 minutes

Preparation
one photocopy, cut up, for each pair of students

Warm-up

1. Bring in some pictures of famous people. Stick them up around the classroom. Ask students to decide who they think is the best-dressed celebrity.
2. Then ask them who they consider to be the best-*looking* celebrity. Ask whether the celebrities in question are successful *because of* how they look or for other reasons. How much did their looks help them to achieve success?

Main activity

1. Students should work in friendship pairs for this activity, or at least with a classmate they know reasonably well. Give each of the pair a different questionnaire.
2. Before they ask their partner the questions, they should predict their partner's answers and write them in the 'Your guesses' column.
3. When they have done this, both students take it in turns to ask and answer the questions. They get a point for every guess that matched their partner's answer.
4. As pairs finish, put them together to form a group of four and ask them to tell each other what they found out about their partners.
5. Now ask each group of four to tell the whole class what they discovered about the members of their group and find out how many points each student got.

Follow-up

- Have a class fashion show with your students. Put students into groups and have one presenter per group. As the students walk up and down the catwalk, the presenter gives a running commentary: *Now we have Sarah, modelling a rather beautiful grey skirt and a highly original white blouse.* Encourage them to use a variety of adjectives.
- Give students copies of magazines or catalogues to cut up. Students work in pairs to produce their ideal man or woman. They can mix features for different people so they may have Brad Pitt's face with David Beckham's body, etc. When their misfit person has been stuck together they can either write about it or simply tell another pair about their creation.
- Either pass the discussion statements below around the class for students to discuss in groups or pairs or use them to hold a class debate.

Discussion statements

You never get a second chance to make a first impression.
If you feel good on the inside, you look good on the outside.
Plastic surgery is dangerous.
People worry too much about what they look like.
Beautiful people have easier lives!
Advertising makes us believe that our appearance is very important.

How well do you know your friend?

Inside-out or not at all?

Give yourself a point for each correct guess.

Before you ask your partner these questions, guess their answers. Then, find out your partner's real answers.

1. Do you agree with the saying 'First impressions count'?
2. What would you wear to go on a first date with someone you really like?
3. If you had the chance to have plastic surgery to improve your looks, would you?
4. How long do you take to get ready to go out at the weekend?
5. Who do you think is the best-looking man in the world?
6. How important is your appearance to you, on a scale of 1–10?
7. Do you think that good-looking people are generally more successful?

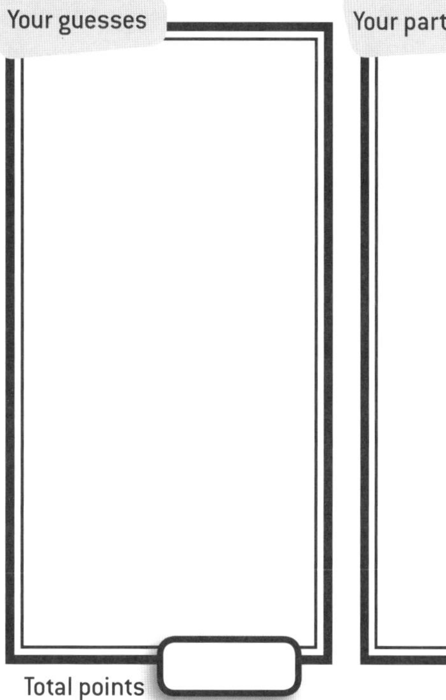
Your guesses
Your partner's answers
Total points

✂ -

How well do you know your friend?

Inside-out or not at all?

Give yourself a point for each correct guess.

Before you ask your partner these questions, guess their answers. Then, find out your partner's real answers.

1. Do you agree with the saying 'Beauty is only skin deep'?
2. What would you wear to meet your boyfriend's / girlfriend's parents for the first time?
3. Would you like to have a tattoo or a piercing?
4. How long do you take to get ready for school in the morning?
5. Who do you think is the best-looking woman in the world?
6. How important is your appearance to you, on a scale of 1–10?
7. Do you believe that it is more acceptable to change some parts of the body by plastic surgery than others?

Your guesses | Your partner's answers

Total points

School alibi

Language focus
question forms, past continuous and past simple

Key vocabulary
innocent, guilty
after-school activities: *listening to music, playing computer games, reading magazines, riding bikes, skateboarding, swimming, training, visiting Granny*

Skills focus
speaking: asking and answering questions

Level
elementary

Time
40 minutes

Preparation
one photocopy, cut up, for each 16 students

Extra notes
If you have more than 16 students in the class, you can have two or more pairs with the same cards. They could either have all been doing the activity together and can work together on their alibis or they can continue to work in pairs.

Warm-up

1. Revise the past continuous tense by getting your students to carry out a mini survey in groups of five to find out what they were doing during the last 24 hours. Draw a table on the board with names along the top row and times going down the first column and ask students to copy it. Students can choose the times they want to put in their survey so they're all different. Students ask one another: *What were you doing at … this morning / last night / yesterday afternoon?*

Names:	**Clara**	
9 o'clock last night	watching TV	

2. Then ask some of the students to tell their findings to the whole class.

Main activity

1. Tell your students that you had a very important envelope full of English exams on your desk after the last class. You left the room at 5.20 pm, went to the staffroom and later realised you'd left the exams behind on your desk. At 5.40 pm you came back to get the exams and they weren't there! Try and bring the scene to life as much as possible by showing your anger at the theft.
2. Tell students that you intend to find out who the guilty students are. Explain that you and your detectives need to know exactly what each of the students was doing at 5.30 pm on the day of the last class.
3. Ask for a third of the class to volunteer to be detectives. They are going to interview the other students to find out who stole the exam papers.
4. Put the rest of the class into pairs. Give each pair a card and tell them that it shows what they were doing after school on the day in question. Both the students in the pair were together at this time and now need to prepare their alibi. The innocent students have a picture of an activity to guide them, but they still need to fill in the details of exactly where they were, who else was there, what they saw, etc. The guilty students have to create their alibi from scratch, so give the guilty cards to two stronger students.
5. Meanwhile, the detectives need to prepare some questions. They may need support with this. Questions could include: *What were you doing at exactly 5.30 pm on the day of the crime?* or *Who were you with?* The detectives should make notes of what they find out as they interview the suspects.
6. Put one detective into a group of three with a pair of suspects. The suspects must be interviewed *individually* to see if their alibi holds up and matches their partner's. If possible, send half the suspects out of the room while their partners are being interviewed. The suspects must not use any notes, they must tell the detective their alibi from memory.
7. When the detective has interviewed both members of the pair separately, they must decide if they think the students are innocent or guilty. All the detectives give their opinion, then ask the guilty suspects to stand up and confess!

Follow-up

- Students can write an article about the crime for the school newspaper.
- Have another round of *Alibi*, changing the roles of the detectives.

7.1 School alibi

1
5.30 pm
2
5.30 pm
3
5.30 pm
4
5.30 pm
5
GIRL
5.30 pm
6
5.30 pm
7
Hello, Gran!
5.30 pm
8
ENGLISH EXAM
5.30 pm

Dodgy dilemmas

Language focus
past continuous and past simple; *should, shouldn't*

Key vocabulary
accident, accidentally, anti-social behaviour, can (noun), *to crash into someone, dodgy, fine* (noun), *to give someone a lift, moustache, old people's home, police officer, punishment, scar, to skateboard, to turn down the music*

Skills focus
reading; speaking: making excuses and giving punishments

Level
intermediate

Time
40 minutes

Preparation
one photocopy, cut up, for each group of 3 to 5 students

Warm-up

1. Write up a table on the board, with headings as in the example below. Ask students to tell you about actions which can get fines in your town or city and fill in the first column of the table on the board.
2. Then put students into pairs or groups to fill in the second column as they think about actions that they believe deserve fines.

FINES ARE GIVEN FOR …	FINES **SHOULD** BE GIVEN FOR …
✔ Smoking on public transport. ✔ Not wearing a seat belt in a car. ✔ Jumping red lights. ✔ Parking in the wrong place.	❍ Dropping rubbish on the floor. ❍ Talking too loudly on mobile phones in public places! ❍ Very noisy motorbikes.

Main activity

1. Put students into groups of between three and five and give each group a situation card and an anti-social behaviour record card.
2. Ask students to read the situation card. Tell them that they are going to act out a role-play with the police officer. Encourage them to elaborate on the situation given and add any more information they like on the back of the card.
3. During the role-play the police officer(s) must decide on the fine or punishment that the behaviour deserves. If the young people manage to convince the police officer that the incident was a 'one-off' event and won't happen again, the police officer may decide not to issue a fine or punishment. Share a few ideas for the punishments, like picking up rubbish for an hour, painting a wall that has graffiti on it or delivering shopping to old people.
4. At this stage, discuss the fact that although they are not serious 'crimes', the policemen are on a mission to reduce anti-social behaviour in the neighbourhood!
5. Students should now decide who is going to take the role of the young people and who is going to take the role of the police officer. You can have up to two police officers and up to three young people per group.
6. To help students you could give a model start to the dialogues such as:
   Police officer: *Hello there. What's going on here?*
   Young person: *Well, I was just …*
   You could also give the police officers certain attitudes you want them to adopt, such as being very strict or being rather soft.
7. Now the students can start to prepare their-role plays. Give the groups time to formulate their ideas and think about the dialogue. They can write out the dialogue first.
8. Students should practise until they are confident enough to either perform their role-play for the whole class or record it.

Follow-up

- Discuss the role of the police force. Offer statements to provoke students' reactions. For example: *The police are very important members of the community,* or *Our town/city would be better without any police.*

7.2 Dodgy dilemmas

Situation One

You were riding your bike and giving a lift to two of your friends. One friend was on the front and one on the seat. You were going quite fast down a hill, when you saw a police officer.

Situation Two

You were drawing on a poster of a very famous politician. You thought she looked better with a moustache, glasses and a scar on her face! You looked up and saw a police officer watching you.

Situation Three

You were playing football on the street next to an old church with special windows. You kicked the ball and accidentally broke one of the ancient windows. You decided to run, but ran straight into a police officer.

Situation Four

You were skateboarding on the pavement in a very busy shopping area of the town centre. You nearly crashed into an old lady, so jumped off your skateboard. The skateboard hit the old lady's legs. Then you saw the police officer.

Situation Five

You were eating a burger and chips in the park with your friends. You didn't see any bins so you all threw your rubbish on the grass. Then you saw the police officer.

Situation Six

You were enjoying the sunshine with your friends, sitting on a bench listening to music. The bench was just outside an old people's home and they had the windows open. The manager asked you to turn the music down but you didn't. Then you saw a police officer.

Anti-social behaviour record card

What happened?

Fine or punishment:

Signature of police:

Anti-social behaviour record card

What happened?

Fine or punishment:

Signature of police:

Anti-social behaviour record card

What happened?

Fine or punishment:

Signature of police:

Anti-social behaviour record card

What happened?

Fine or punishment:

Signature of police:

Anti-social behaviour record card

What happened?

Fine or punishment:

Signature of police:

Anti-social behaviour record card

What happened?

Fine or punishment:

Signature of police:

Crime controversy

Language focus
relative clauses, present simple, crime

Key vocabulary
justice and punishment: *capital punishment, community service, controversy, crime, to go to court, jail, judge, jury, to serve a prison sentence*

Skills focus
speaking: describing, persuading
reading: answering questions

Level
upper-intermediate

Time
50 minutes

Preparation
one set of cards for each group of 4 students; one photocopy of the questionnaire for each student

Warm-up

1. You may need to revise language of agreeing and disagreeing and language of persuasion before starting the main activity.
2. Bring in a newspaper article about a local criminal case that your students will have heard about. Talk about the case and ask for your students' opinions of it. Use this opportunity to check students' understanding of the key vocabulary needed in the activity. For example, ask students *Do you think X should do community service or serve a prison sentence for the crime?*

Main activity

1. Put students into groups of four. Give each group one set of word cards: half the cards to one pair and half to the other pair. The two pairs in the group play against each other and take it in turns to try and define the word at the top of each card *without* using any of the three words below. Set a time limit of a minute or two. If they guess the target word, they win the card. The winners are the pair with the most cards.
2. Now move on to the questionnaire and give each student a copy. Students now work in pairs. First of all they should read the sentences carefully and think, on their own, about whether or not they agree or disagree with the statement, and to what extent. They should write their answers (1–5 according to the scale at the top of the questionnaire) in the box in the YOU column.
3. When students have completed the YOU column, they should compare and share their answers with their partner and complete the YOUR PARTNER column. Where there is a difference in opinion, students should express their views as clearly as possible and justify their opinions with their reasons. Students should try and persuade their partner to change their original view. Whether or not they change their view, they should write their 'new opinion', which may well be the same as their original opinion, in the third YOU – ON REFLECTION column.
4. When all the pairs have finished, ask the class who changed their views following a discussion with their partner for at least one of the statements. Ask them to explain their change of opinion to the class.

Follow-up

- Use one of the statements (the one that caused the most controversy) for a class debate.
- Students write two more controversial statements about crime and justice. They can now localise the statements by mentioning the local police force or a recent well publicised criminal case.
- Ask your students to think of criminal cases that may be heard in court and to write one each on a piece of paper. Collect them all in. Use the best cases to do role-plays. Put students into groups or between four and six, nominate one judge, one criminal and a small jury (between two and four students) and ask them to role play the scene at court. The jury should decide on an appropriate punishment for the crime.

7.3 Crime controversy

Word cards

Prison sentence	Community service	Capital punishment	Jail
› time › jail › punishment	› work › neighbourhood › punishment	› kill › prisoner › death row	› prison › cells › locked up
Court	**Judge**	**Jury**	**Police force**
› justice › judge › criminals	› court › uniform › decision / to decide	› citizens › decision / to decide › guilty	› police officer › uniform › law

Questionnaire

1 – Completely disagree
2 – Mainly disagree
3 – Neither agree nor disagree
4 – Mainly agree
5 – Completely agree

	YOU	YOUR PARTNER	YOU – ON REFLECTION
a Serving a prison sentence can't change the character of a criminal.			
b Community service is a better punishment than a prison sentence for most crimes.			
c Capital punishment is fair in clear and deliberate murder cases. 'An eye for an eye, a tooth for a tooth.'			
d Under-eighteens who commit crimes should receive exactly the same punishment as adults.			
e Prisoners are treated too well in jail.			
f The police force do an extremely important job.			
g Rich and influential people have more privileges in court.			
h Judges and juries are always right and their opinions should be respected.			

Superhero comic strip

Language focus
can/can't to express abilities, direct speech

Key vocabulary
informal speech of the comic characters – student generated

Skills focus
writing a comic strip story

Level
elementary

Time
60 minutes

Preparation
one photocopy for each student (or two copies each, so they can use one for their first draft); (optional) favourite comics or graphic novels brought in by students or by you

Warm-up

- Use the picture of the superteacher (below) to give students some ideas of superpowers, for example X-ray eyes to catch cheats. Then ask them to think of other powers that superheroes may have. Make a list on the board.

Main activity

1. Ask your students if they think the superteacher they've just seen would be successful if published in a comic.
2. Ask your students if they think they could design a popular superhero for a new comic. Give the photocopy of a blank cartoon strip to each student and allow them about ten minutes to design their superhero. They should complete the details on the left about their superhero and make a quick sketch of their hero below. Students could work in pairs for this activity.
3. Give students time to think of an opening sequence for a comic strip featuring their superhero. Offer ideas and language input and if you have examples of comics or graphic novels, let students have a look at them. If you prefer, set a location for all the students to use, such as your town centre or school.
4. Support students as they write their comic strips and encourage them to map out their comic in rough and do all the writing before they begin drawing.
5. Display the finished comic strips around the class so that all the students can read each others' work. You could hold a class vote to see which of the comic strips the class thinks are the best.
6. Alternatively, ask students to present their superhero and comic strip to the class. Hold a class vote on which heroes you think a comic designer would accept.

Follow-up

- Put all the students' comic strips together to make a comic magazine. Give the job of creating the cover to some of the students who finish their comic strips early. Display the finished result on a notice board.
- Find out who the comic fans are in your class and ask them to bring in some of their favourite comics. Make small groups with a comic fan in each and ask the others to ask the fans some questions about the characters and the comic.

Superpen – can mark 100 exams in one minute
X-ray eyes – can see cheats
Superhand – can photocopy without a photocopier

8.1 Superhero comic strip

Boom!
whew!
ZAPP!
Kaput!
POW!
My Superhero
Name:
Appearance:
Superpowers:
Picture:

Heroic sketches

Language focus
narrative tenses

Key vocabulary
hero, heroine, location, superpower, villain
students' own input

Skills focus
writing: storytelling
speaking: performing a sketch

Level
intermediate

Time
90 minutes

Preparation
one photocopy and one dice for each group of 4 to 7 students

Extra notes
This activity could be developed into a whole project. Students could make props and dress up. You could film the performances. Students write a review of their favourite sketch.

Warm-up

1. Play a quick game of Hangman to get the word SUPERHERO on the board.
2. When the word appears, ask students what they think about when they see the word *superhero,* and draw a mind map around the word. Ensure the word *villain* is elicited and introduced at this stage.

Main activity

1. Put students into groups of between four and seven and give one activity sheet to each group. Tell the students that they are going to use the activity sheet to help them decide on the main ingredients for a short sketch or play.
2. Go through the column headings and elicit some examples of each. The heroes and villains can be 'real' (from films or comics) or made up. Then give each group ten minutes to think of six possibilities for each column and write them in.
3. When the table is full, give each group a dice and ask them to throw it to decide on the element to be chosen in each column. For example, the first throw chooses which superhero, the second throw which villain, and so on. As they throw the dice they should circle the chosen words.
4. When they have thrown the dice six times they will have selected the six 'ingredients' for their sketch (a very short play).
5. Now tell the students that they are going to use the selected 'ingredients' to write a short sketch which incorporates them all. Choose one of the stronger students in each group to be the Narrator. They can decide themselves who is going to play the other roles and write this on the activity sheet. The Narrator's role is to give a commentary on the action and to fill in any gaps in the plot.
6. Set a time limit and offer advice and support for students to create a three- or four-minute superhero sketch. They can base their ideas on a film or comic scenario. Students should write out the dialogue in their groups first and then perform with or without notes.
7. When the groups are ready, you could either film the performances or ask each group to perform live for the rest of the class. As the groups watch, they should try and remember the location, the names of the heroes and villains and the special objects that are used. At the end, ask the class about each sketch, for example: *Where was the location? Who was the villain?* etc.

Follow-up

- Students write a review of one of the sketches they saw.
- Imagine the sketches were scenes from a film. Students develop their ideas into a film. They should think of the cast, choosing the actors they'd like to play each role, and think about how the sketch could be developed into a blockbuster.
- Students interview the actors of the sketches as if they're giving a promotional interview for television.
- Make the sketches into comic strips. Or if you have the resources, you could take photos of the characters in action to make a photo story. These could be displayed on the wall or made into computer presentations.

8.2 Heroic sketches

	Superhero	Villain	Location	Object	Main event	Ending
	Example: Super T.J.	Bad Boy Beastie	Rio de Janeiro	ice sword	bank robbery	hero and villain fall in love

Superhero:	**Played by:**	**Villain:**	**Played by:**
Narrator:	**Played by:**	**Other characters:**	**Played by:**

Title:

Summary of plot:

Real-life heroes

Language focus
present simple, conditionals, *should*, jobs

Key vocabulary
daily routines and heroic acts specific to the following occupations:
aid worker, environmental activist, farmer, firefighter, human rights campaigner, medical researcher, police officer, psychiatrist, self-made millionaire, soldier, surgeon

Skills focus
speaking: justifying and persuading

Level
upper-intermediate

Time
45 minutes

Preparation
photocopies, cut up into cards, one card for each student, enough so that each job is held by at least 2 students

Warm-up

1. Ask students if they agree or disagree with the following statements:
   Heroes only exist in films and comics.
   Real heroes must have superpowers.
   Heroes exist in real life and can be normal people.
   I have a hero.
   I think I am a hero sometimes!

   Students can show their responses by putting up their hands, or by standing up if they agree. Or they could write down their responses and then just share their opinions with a partner.
2. Alternatively, if there has been a recent heroic event in your local community such as someone being saved from a fire, or volunteers cleaning up a dirty beach, use this event to introduce the idea of real-life heroes.

Main activity

1. Ask students if they think certain jobs are more heroic than others and why. Ask them to think of some jobs they consider heroic.
2. Give students a job card each, then put all the students with the same card together. If you have a small class, use only a selection of the job cards so that there are at least two students with each job card. Ask students to think about how this job might be heroic.
3. Now ask students in their groups to create a profile for an imaginary person who does the job on their card. They could base their ideas on people who they've heard about in the news, or on famous people they know about, or they can invent a character. They can make extra notes on the back of their cards.
4. When all the students have completed their profiles, it's time to mix up the groups so they now contain a selection of jobs. If you have a very big class, you may decide to make groups of seven, eight or nine, but five or six is probably a better size. As long as each group is made up of students with different jobs, it doesn't matter.
5. Students use their completed profiles as the basis for a role-play of the classic 'Hot Air Balloon Debate'. Set the scene that the group is travelling in a hot air balloon over shark-infested waters. (Drawing on the board will help.) Tell students that there isn't enough gas to reach land so the group should decide on one or two people that they are going to throw overboard in order to save the others. Each person should argue why their job is the most important in order to save their own life. Set a time limit for students to argue it out!
6. When all the groups have finished, ask for class feedback to see who was chosen in each group to be thrown out of the balloon.

Follow-up

- Students write a day-in-the-life article for the character's blog or diary. They could describe a typical day or a particularly heroic day.
- Use the job profiles to write newspaper articles about heroic acts carried out by the characters the students have created. The tales of heroism could be serious or quite ridiculous if you want to add a fun element to the writing.
- In pairs, one student is the hero and one the interviewer; they prepare a short interview for a new TV programme called 'Real-Life Heroes'.

8.3 Real-life heroes

Human rights campaigner	Firefighter	Medical researcher
Name: ______	Name: ______	Name: ______
Day-to-day work: ______ ______	Day-to-day work: ______ ______	Day-to-day work: ______ ______
Special achievements: ______ ______	Special achievements: ______ ______	Special achievements: ______ ______
Surgeon	**Teacher**	**Aid worker**
Name: ______	Name: ______	Name: ______
Day-to-day work: ______ ______	Day-to-day work: ______ ______	Day-to-day work: ______ ______
Special achievements: ______ ______	Special achievements: ______ ______	Special achievements: ______ ______
Farmer	**Police officer**	**Soldier**
Name: ______	Name: ______	Name: ______
Day-to-day work: ______ ______	Day-to-day work: ______ ______	Day-to-day work: ______ ______
Special achievements: ______ ______	Special achievements: ______ ______	Special achievements: ______ ______
Environmental activist	**Self-made millionaire**	**Psychiatrist**
Name: ______	Name: ______	Name: ______
Day-to-day work: ______ ______	Day-to-day work: ______ ______	Day-to-day work: ______ ______
Special achievements: ______ ______	Special achievements: ______ ______	Special achievements: ______ ______

Footie stars

Language focus
comparatives: *better, more/less ... than*; questions in the present and past simple

Key vocabulary
football language: *coach, injury, international title, mascot, red card, to score a goal*
high numbers: *a million, a thousand*

Skills focus
speaking: asking questions and comparing information

Level
elementary

Time
45 minutes

Preparation
one photocopy, cut up, for each pair of students

Warm-up

- Ask students which football teams they support, who their favourite footballers are, etc. As you're talking to them, pre-teach the vocabulary necessary for the game (see Key vocabulary) and write it on the board. Get students to tell you how much footballers earn. Pre-teach the high numbers students will need to do this task: millions and thousands.

Main activity

1. Show students one of the cards as an example and check their understanding of the categories: *International titles, Goals scored last season, Cost, Injuries* and *Red cards.*
2. Ask students to ask you questions about the categories regarding the footballer you have on your card. Elicit the following questions and ask students whether it's good to have a high number or a low number. Explain whether it's the highest or lowest statistic that wins.
   How many international titles does he have? – **highest** figure wins
   How many goals did he score last season? – **highest** figure wins
   How much did he cost? – **highest** figure wins
   How many injuries did he have last year? – **lowest** figure wins
   How many red cards did he get? – **lowest** figure wins
3. Demonstrate the game with you and one student before the students begin to play in pairs. In order to win, students should try and have the best statistic in a certain category. If both have the same number for that category on their card, the questioner must ask another question so that every round has a winner. Make it clear during the demonstration that the students must ask proper questions and the player with the winning card should react to the result by using a sentence with a comparative, in order to win their opponent's card. For example:

   A: *How many goals did your player score last season?*
   B: *Two.*
   A: *My player is better. He scored seven goals last season, so I win the card!*
   or
   A: *How much did your player cost?*
   B: *Nineteen million dollars.*
   A: *My player only cost eighty thousand.*
   B: *So my player was more expensive. I win!*
4. The aim of the game is to win as many cards as possible by always choosing the statistic that you think will beat your opponent. If any of the language needed to play the game is new to the students, write it up on the board as support.
5. Give a set of cards to each pair of students. They shuffle the cards and deal them face down to each player. They each turn over their top card and play until one of the pair wins all the cards. Then they shuffle the cards well and play again. As students play, monitor carefully and support weaker students if necessary until they get the idea.

Follow-up

- Choose another topic of interest and ask students to create their own set of cards.
- Students make a poster version of a similar card for their favourite football player to display. They could find the statistics they need on the Internet.

9.1 Footie stars

GAZZO
Goalkeeper
- International titles: 4
- Goals scored last season: 0
- Cost: $24,000,000
- Injuries: 3
- Red cards: 0

PABLO
Centre back
- International titles: 1
- Goals scored last season: 0
- Cost: $16,000,000
- Injuries: 2
- Red cards: 5

GIOVANI
Left back
- International titles: 3
- Goals scored last season: 1
- Cost: $18,000,000
- Injuries: 1
- Red cards: 2

PAOLINHO
Right back
- International titles: 2
- Goals scored last season: 2
- Cost: $22,000,000
- Injuries: 3
- Red cards: 4

ZIGGÁ
Centre back
- International titles: 5
- Goals scored last season: 3
- Cost: $24,000,000
- Injuries: 4
- Red cards: 2

TOTÓ
Centre forward
- International titles: 6
- Goals scored last season: 29
- Cost: $31,000,000
- Injuries: 6
- Red cards: 3

DAN
Centre forward
- International titles: 7
- Goals scored last season: 23
- Cost: $32,000,000
- Injuries: 3
- Red cards: 2

CLANCY
Centre midfield
- International titles: 8
- Goals scored last season: 35
- Cost: $40,000,000
- Injuries: 3
- Red cards: 1

MICHAEL
Right midfield
- International titles: 0
- Goals scored last season: 8
- Cost: $19,000,000
- Injuries: 1
- Red cards: 4

BAB-NOOSH
Left midfield
- International titles: 1
- Goals scored last season: 14
- Cost: $25,000,000
- Injuries: 2
- Red cards: 0

BOOTIE
Centre forward
- International titles: 2
- Goals scored last season: 10
- Cost: $28,000,000
- Injuries: 3
- Red cards: 2

JONATHAN
Centre midfield
- International titles: 0
- Goals scored last season: 4
- Cost: $2,000,000
- Injuries: 0
- Red cards: 0

RICE
Right midfield
- International titles: 3
- Goals scored last season: 5
- Cost: $13,000,000
- Injuries: 0
- Red cards: 0

KEVIN
Left midfield
- International titles: 4
- Goals scored last season: 6
- Cost: $12,000,000
- Injuries: 0
- Red cards: 4

McGRATH
Coach
- International titles: 9
- Goals scored last season: 0
- Cost: $80,000
- Injuries: 0
- Red cards: 1

CHARLIE-CHAMPO
Club mascot
- International titles: 6
- Goals scored last season: 0
- Cost: free!
- Injuries: 0
- Red cards: 1

Sports reporters

Language focus
question forms

Key vocabulary
sports (depending on students' choice of sports star)

Skills focus
speaking: asking and answering questions, and summarising information; listening; writing: note taking

Level
intermediate

Time
60 minutes

Preparation
one photocopy and a sticky label for each student

Extra notes
Although this can be noisy, it is a great way to carry out structured role-play. As students repeat the interview four times with different partners, their confidence will grow as the activity progresses.

Warm-up

1. Read out the sentences below. Tell students that when they hear a sentence that is true for them, they should stand up. In a small group, students could stand in a line and step forward if the statement is true and back if it's false.
   I love watching sports on TV.
   I would like to be a professional footballer / tennis player / basketball player.
   (Choose sports you know your students love.)
   I like/hate playing sports.
   I have a favourite sports star.
2. Add some sentences of your own about popular sports stars or local teams.

Main activity

1. Tell students they are going to be sports journalists and interview several sports stars for a sports magazine. Unfortunately they don't know exactly who they are going to interview, so they have to think of five questions that they could ask any sports stars. For example: *What's the best thing about being a sports star? What are your ambitions for this year? What was the best moment in your career?* Give out the activity sheets and ask students to write their five questions in the *Questions* column.
2. Give each student a sticky label and ask them to write the name of their favourite sports star on it, and to stick it on themselves.
3. Tell students that they are going to take on the role of sports journalist *and* their chosen sports star for this activity.
4. Make two concentric circles. Half the class form the inner circle, facing the other half of the class, who form the outer circle, facing inwards. Students need to bring with them the activity sheet, a pen and a book to lean on. If space is limited, they can just stand up and mingle.
5. When students are in position, tell them that they will have three minutes to interview the sports star opposite them and to be interviewed themselves. Pairs can decide who is interviewed first. When you say *Stop and change* they must stop talking *immediately*.
6. Be sure to keep the partner changes snappy. At three-minute intervals, shout *Stop and change*. The outer circle should take a step to the right to change partners. If students are just mingling, make sure everybody ends up with a new partner.
7. As students are carrying out the interviews they should make a note of their partner's answers in the table. Encourage them to really get into the role of their chosen sports star and to invent any answers they don't know.
8. After four rounds of interviews all students should have completed their tables. Ask a few individuals to tell the class what they discovered.

Follow-up

- Students write an article for a sports magazine about one or more of the stars they interviewed. They could find photos on the Internet to include.
- If you have access to a computer room, students can check the information they were given during the interviews against the true information.
- Students make a radio programme by recording the interviews.

9.2 Sports reporters

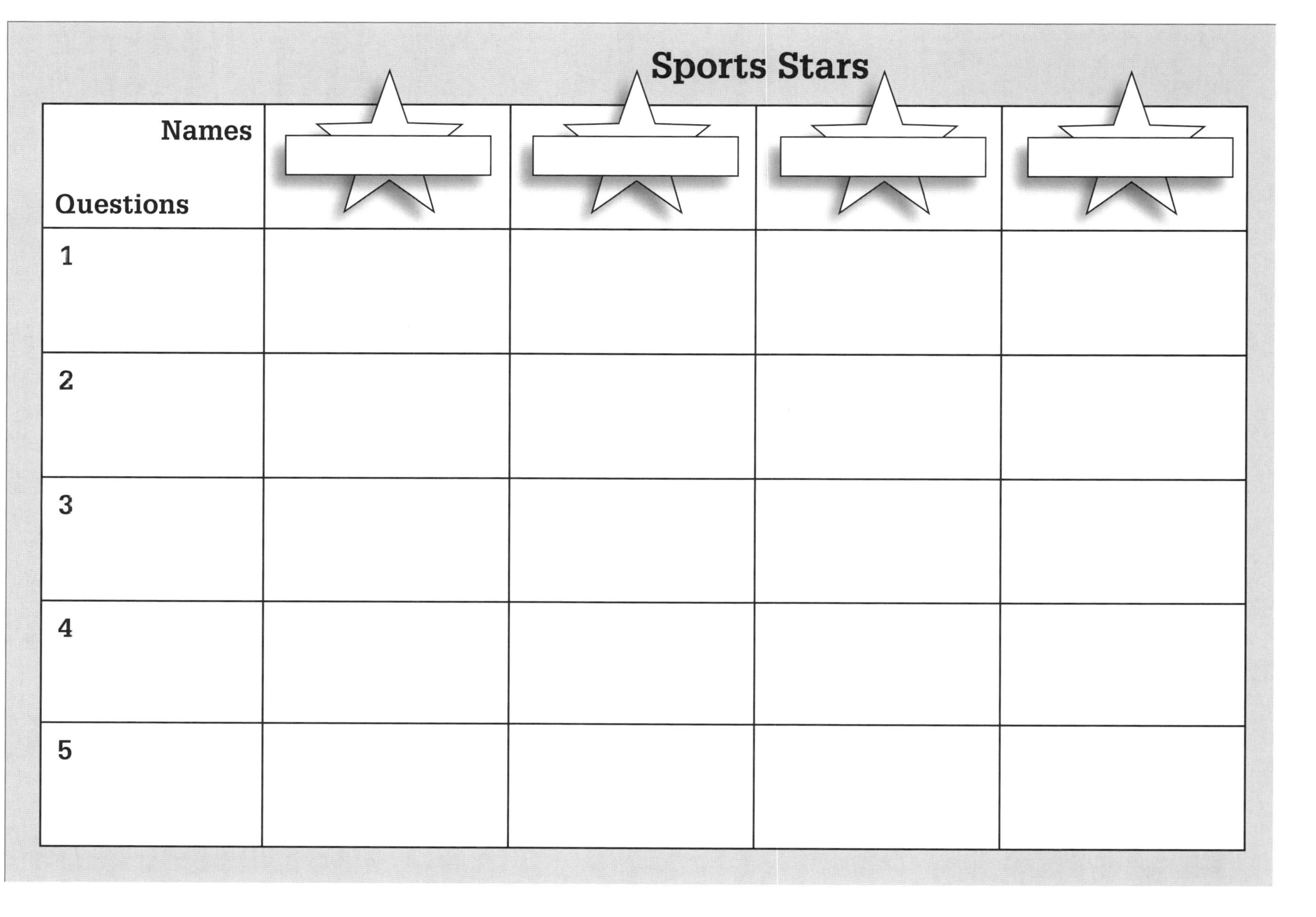

Sports Stars

Names / Questions				
1				
2				
3				
4				
5				

Sports quiz

Language focus
question forms

Key vocabulary
breathing apparatus, dimple, goggles, polo, race, referee, score, snooker, synchronised swimming, target, tournament, track, umpire

Skills focus
speaking: answering questions

Level
upper-intermediate

Time
50 minutes

Preparation
one photocopy, cut up, per class; a piece of scrap paper for each team of 3 to 6 students

Warm-up

- Put students into pairs facing their partner for the word association game Vocabulary Tennis. Give them a key word. Students say a word connected to the key word, then their partner should say another word that is linked to the previous word, and so on until one of them repeats a word that has already been said, or can't think of a word to add. For example:

Teacher:	*Football*		
Student A:	*Goal*	Student B:	*Player*
Student A:	*Referee*	Student B:	*Coach*
Student A:	*Training*	Student B:	*Ball*
Student A:	*Kick*	Student B:	*Mmmmm ...*
Student A:	*I win!*		

Key words to start each round should be connected to the world of sports, such as *swimming pool, Olympics, tennis, sports centre, water sports*, etc.

Main activity

1. Divide the class into between three and six teams and ask them to think of a team name. Try to mix up the students who you know are keen on sports with those who are less interested.
2. Give each team a piece of scrap paper and ask them to write their team name on the top and to put numbers 1–8 down the side.
3. Ask for a volunteer student to be the Quizmaster, maybe someone who's not very keen on sport, to read the Round 1 questions out one by one (but NB not the answers, which are in italics!), or you can read them yourself. Give the teams enough time to consult amongst themselves and write down their answer. Encourage the students to always guess an answer if they're not sure.
4. At the end of the round, ask the teams to pass their answer papers to another team and go through the answers so they can mark each others' papers. The Quizmaster reads out the correct answers. Students should write a clear score on the bottom of the answer sheet before handing it back to the team.
5. Decide how many rounds to play, depending on how much time you have and if students are still enjoying the quiz. After each round ask the teams their scores and keep a running total on the board. The winning team could win a small prize or they could leave the class first.
6. If you want to add a photo round, bring in photos of famous sports people and ask students to name the person and the sport for a bonus point.

Follow-up

- Students prepare rounds of quizzes on other topics, for example, the natural world, music, celebrities, films, TV, etc. Mix the topics and have a giant quiz on the last day of term or on a special occasion. You could also have quizzes that work in the same way to revise language covered during the course. If students prepare the questions when it's their round, they become the Quizmasters and don't take part in that round. As long as each team sits out one round to ask their own questions, the results will be fair.

9.3 Sports quiz

Sports quiz – Round 1

1 Which is the only Grand Slam tennis tournament played on grass? *Wimbledon*
2 Where was the game of golf invented? *Scotland*
3 Name a water sport that is only done by women. *Synchronised swimming*
4 What do the five interlinked Olympic rings on the flag represent? *The five continents*
5 Which sport has four different colour codes for the balls, depending on the speed of the ball? *Squash*
6 Name three sports where gloves are worn. *e.g. golf, boxing, baseball, cycling, football (goalkeeper)*
7 What do you call the special glasses you wear for swimming? *Goggles*
8 What do Americans call the game that in the UK is called 'football'? *Soccer*

Sports quiz – Round 2

1 Which two British universities race against each other in an annual boat race? *Oxford and Cambridge*
2 In golf, what does 'par' mean? *'Par' is the target score for an individual hole.*
3 In basketball, what does NBA stand for? *National Basketball Association*
4 How many red balls are there in snooker? *15*
5 How many players are there in a cricket team? *11*
6 Name three sports that use nets. *e.g. tennis, football, volleyball, basketball, badminton*
7 In football, what's the name of the person who keeps the game under control and applies the rules? *The referee*
8 Exactly how long is a marathon? *42.195 kilometres or 26 miles 385 yards* (Team with closest guess wins.)

Sports quiz – Round 3

1 What's the name of the sport where you dive as deep as you possibly can without breathing apparatus? *Free diving*
2 Which of these sports is not an Olympic sport: boxing, golf, kayaking, mountain biking? *Golf*
3 There are twelve players in a golf Ryder Cup team. True or false? *True*
4 Why was the football World Cup not held in 1942 and 1946? *Because of World War 2*
5 What colour belt comes after white in judo? *Yellow*
6 Name three sports where you need wheels. *e.g. motor racing, cycling, motorbike racing, rollerblading*
7 In which sporting race does the winner wear a yellow T-shirt? *Cycling* (*the Tour de France*)
8 What sports are included in a triathlon? *Swimming, cycling, running*

Sports quiz – Round 4

1 How high is a basketball net? *3 metres*
2 Name a water sport that has the same name as a sport played on horses. *Polo*
3 In which sport does the winner get a green jacket? *Golf* (*the US Masters*)
4 There are 250 dimples on a golf ball. True or false? *False – most balls have 300–450 dimples*
5 In which sport do players take long and short corners? *Hockey*
6 Name three racket sports. *e.g. tennis, badminton, paddle, squash*
7 In the UK the Grand National is a very famous race. What type of race is it? *A horse race*
8 In tennis what's the name of the person who keeps score and applies the rules? *The umpire*

Shopping spree

Language focus
functional shopping language

Key vocabulary
prices and shopping

Skills focus
speaking: asking prices, buying and selling

Level
elementary

Time
60 minutes

Preparation
one copy of the money board for each pair of students; one or more sets (depending on the size of the class) of product cards, cut up

Warm-up

1. Put students into pairs and give them a copy of the top part of the activity sheet. Ask them to read each sentence and decide whether it would be spoken by a shop assistant or a customer.
2. Check answers and get students to practise saying the sentences aloud.
3. Ask them in their pairs to create a simple shopping dialogue, using some of the sentences. Ask several pairs to read their dialogues to the class.

Main activity

1. Put students in groups of four and tell them they're going to go shopping but first they have to win some money to spend. Students should take it in turns to close their eyes and mark three dots on the money board on their activity sheet. Then they calculate how much they have won. This is how much they can spend during the role-play.
2. Choose a shop assistant for each shop – the trainer shop, the electrical shop and the bag shop. In a large class, have six assistants, two for each shop. Give each assistant all the product cards for their shop and ask them to set up their shop on a table by folding the item cards so that the price, size and colour information is facing them, and the picture of the product is facing the customers.
3. The shoppers have to spend their money as wisely as possible, buying the items they really like with the money they have available. When a shopper purchases an item, the shop assistant should give them the product card, so some items may sell out. The shoppers should keep a note of how much they are spending to make sure they don't go over their budget. Set a time limit.
4. Encourage shoppers to talk to each other while they're waiting to be served. You could join in too to encourage this type of interaction. As you are mingling amongst them, make a note of good language you hear and also any frequent mistakes. Use this to give feedback at the end.
5. When the shopping spree is over, ask students what they bought, why they chose the items and how much money they have left. The fact that all the students had different amounts to spend should lead to some interesting discussion and you can ask students how they go about saving money to buy things they really want.

Follow-up

- Collect images of new products your students will be interested in, such as MP3 players, mobile phones, clothes, etc. Show the items to students and get them to guess how much each item costs. Then, divide students into groups and tell the students they have a set amount of money. Calculate the amount so they have enough to buy several items, but not all of them, at their real price. Then auction off the goods to the groups. Students can bid for items but can't spend over their budget. The aim of the game is for students to make a profit and buy the goods at below their market price. They should try not to spend more money than they think the goods are worth. At the end of the auction, show students the prices for the goods and get them to work out how much money they've made or lost.

10.1 Shopping spree

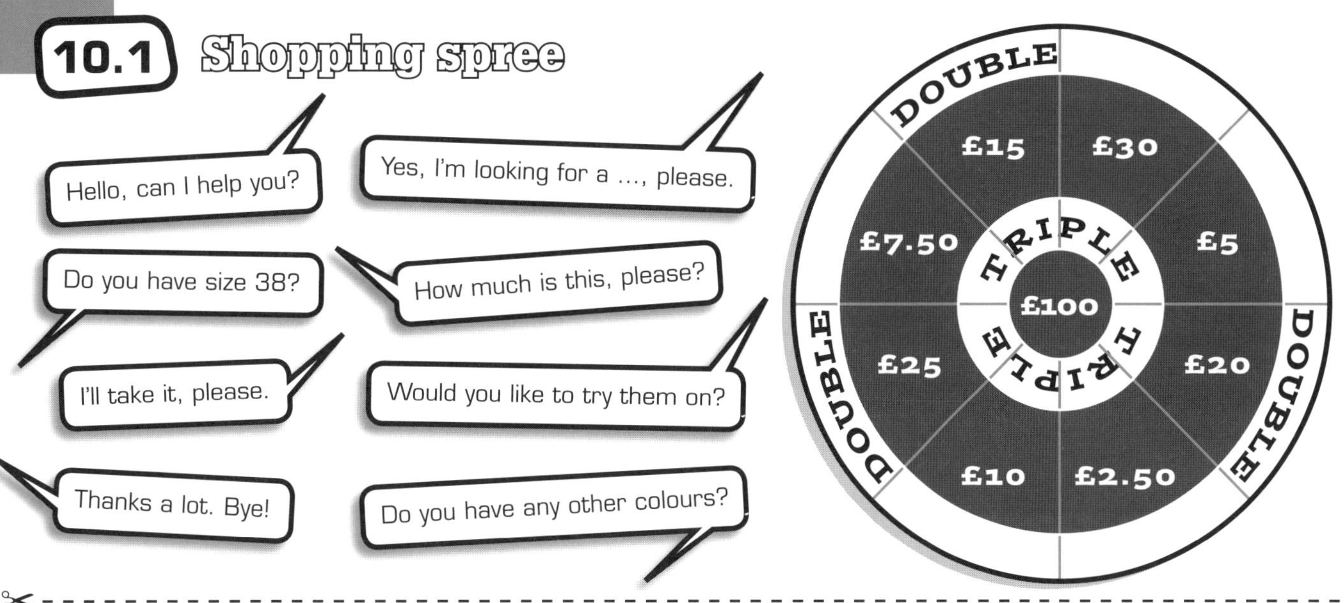

Hello, can I help you?
Yes, I'm looking for a ..., please.
Do you have size 38?
How much is this, please?
I'll take it, please.
Would you like to try them on?
Thanks a lot. Bye!
Do you have any other colours?
DOUBLE
£15
£30
£7.50
£5
TRIPLE
£100
TRIPLE
DOUBLE
£25
£20
DOUBLE
£10
£2.50

Product cards

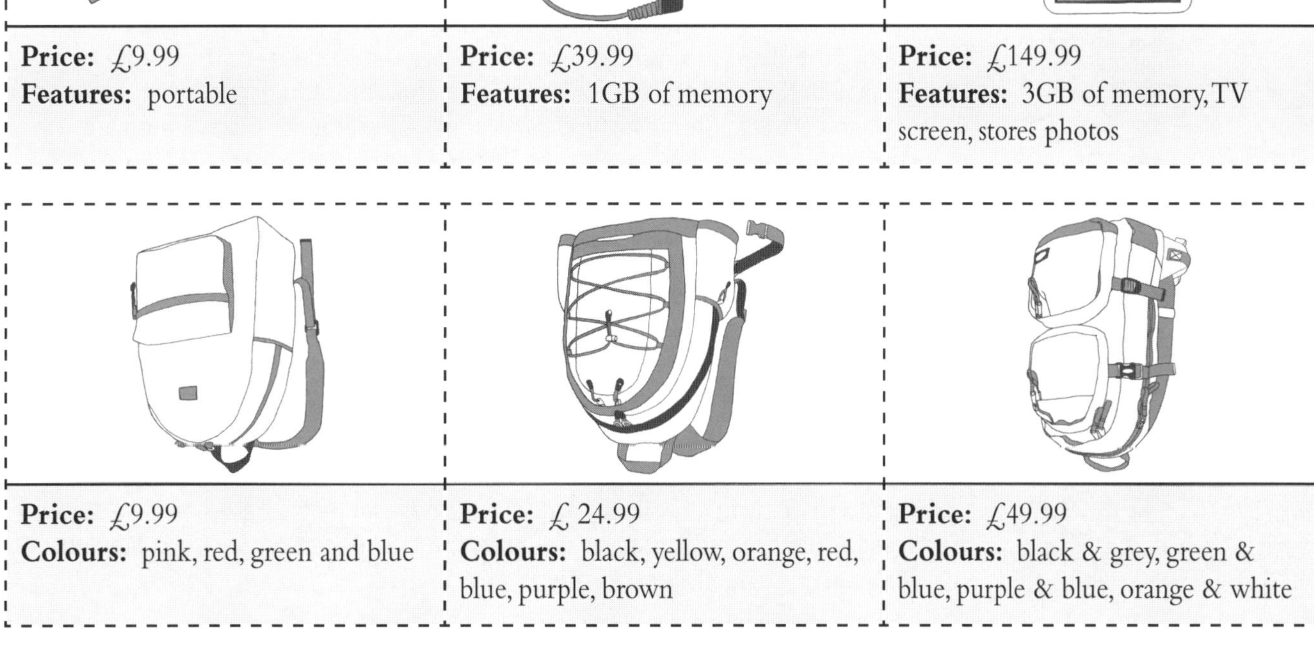

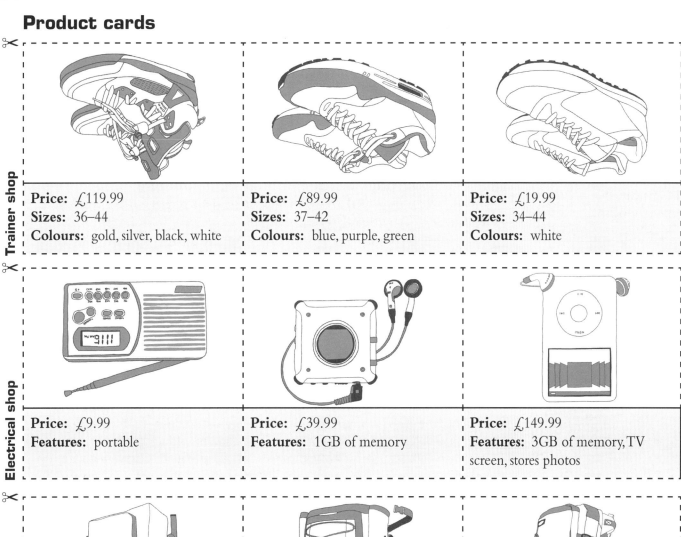

Trainer shop

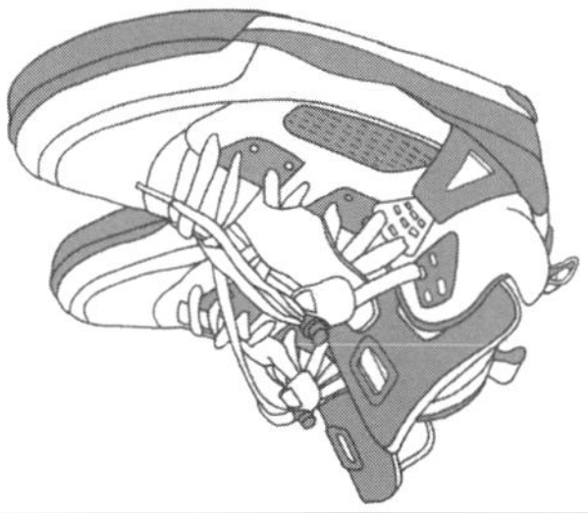 **Price:** £119.99 **Sizes:** 36–44 **Colours:** gold, silver, black, white	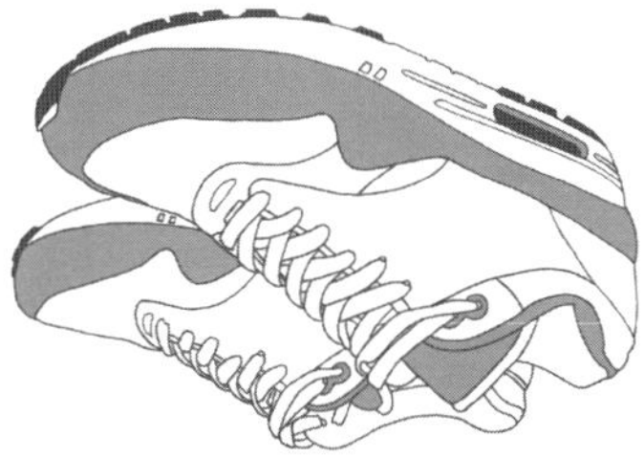 **Price:** £89.99 **Sizes:** 37–42 **Colours:** blue, purple, green	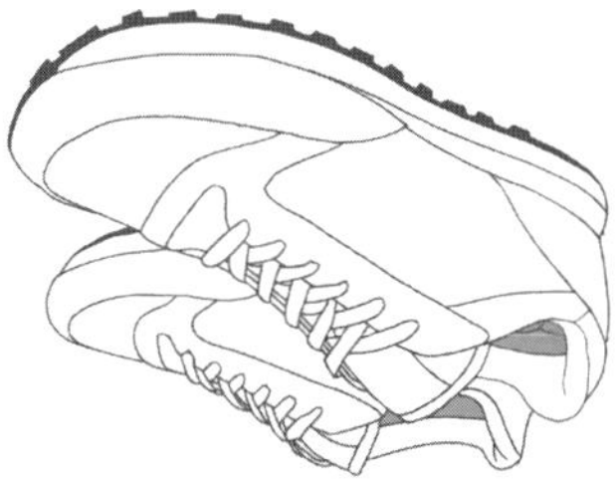 **Price:** £19.99 **Sizes:** 34–44 **Colours:** white

Electrical shop

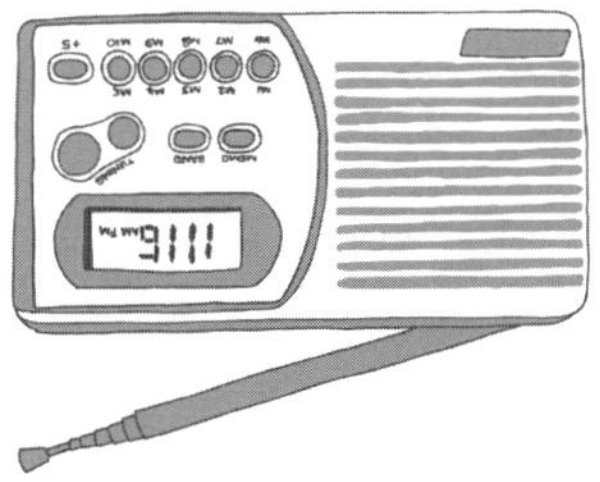 **Price:** £9.99 **Features:** portable	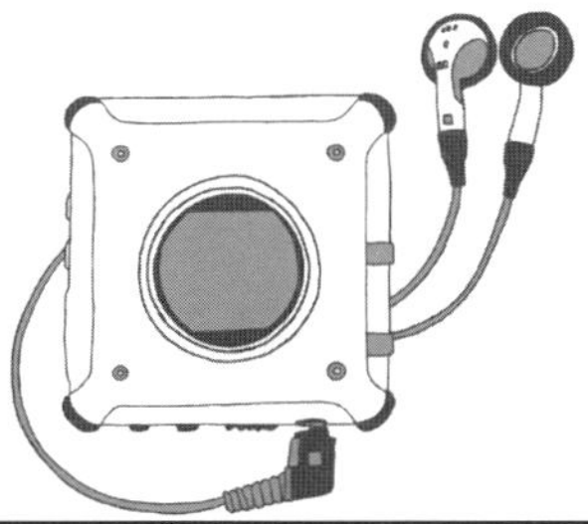 **Price:** £39.99 **Features:** 1GB of memory	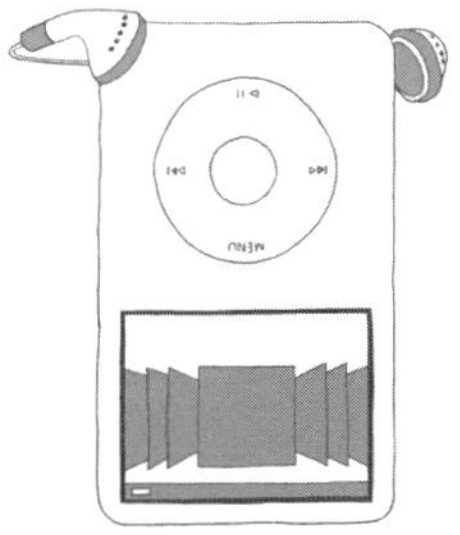 **Price:** £149.99 **Features:** 3GB of memory, TV screen, stores photos

Bag shop

Price: £9.99 **Colours:** pink, red, green and blue	**Price:** £ 24.99 **Colours:** black, yellow, orange, red, blue, purple, brown	**Price:** £49.99 **Colours:** black & grey, green & blue, purple & blue, orange & white

The real cost

Language focus
present simple and past simple passives

Key vocabulary
prices and business language: *advertising, brand, credit cards, materials, material world, production, profit, quality, rent, tax, VAT, wages, waste of money*

Skills focus
speaking: discussing and comparing, expressing opinions

Level
intermediate

Time
60 minutes

Preparation
one photocopy, cut up, for each pair of students

Warm-up

1. Ask students to have a look at the labels on their clothes, bags, etc. and to tell you where they were made. Ask them if they ever think about where their clothes (or other items) were made and who made them.
2. You could now ask students what factors they consider when they shop for a new item of clothing: price? colour? quality? Ask students how important it is for them to buy the fashionable brand names. This topic often leads into an interesting discussion with teenagers.

Main activity

1. Put students into pairs or small groups and give each the top part of the activity sheet with the trainer on. Ask students how much this pair of trainers costs (€100). Ask students if they think that's a fair price for a pair of trainers.
2. Now, explain to students that around the picture are the different things that make up the whole cost of the trainers. To teach the new language give a definition or clue and ask the students to look at the activity sheet to guess the word. For example: *the money you pay to live in a house or to use a shop – rent,* etc.
3. Ask students to match the figures in the box to the cost areas. Some have already been completed for them. Encourage them to use the passive: *I think €3 is spent on transport and tax.*
4. Ask groups to compare their answers or compare them as a whole class.
5. Then give students the answers. The most surprising is often the wages of the shoemaker, only €0.50. Use this fact to talk about 'fair trade' products, where producers get a fair amount of money for their work or for the raw materials they produce.

Answers
1 €3 2 €1.50 3 €5 4 €0.50 5 €18 6 €8.50 7 €13

6. Now mix students into different groups of about four. Cut up the discussion statements and give each group one strip to discuss for a few minutes before rotating the strips around the groups. Encourage students to think about the message behind the statement and to give their opinions on whether or not they agree with it. Monitor the groups carefully and feed in new language when necessary. Finish the class by hearing some of the students' views on the statements.

Follow-up

- If you have access to the Internet, use a search engine to find more information about the topic of fair trade. Type 'fair trade' or 'clean clothes' into a search engine and ask students to skim read some web pages to find out more.
- Ask students to think of their own original quote about the topic of consumerism. They could write the quotes onto card or coloured paper to create a display on a notice board. The quotes can be very simple. Give some ideas to start your students off, for example 'Think before you buy.' 'Don't buy what you don't need.' 'Less is more!'
- Students design a poster to encourage their peers to think before they buy.

10.2 The real cost

€18 €1.50 €0.50 €5 €3 €8.50 €13

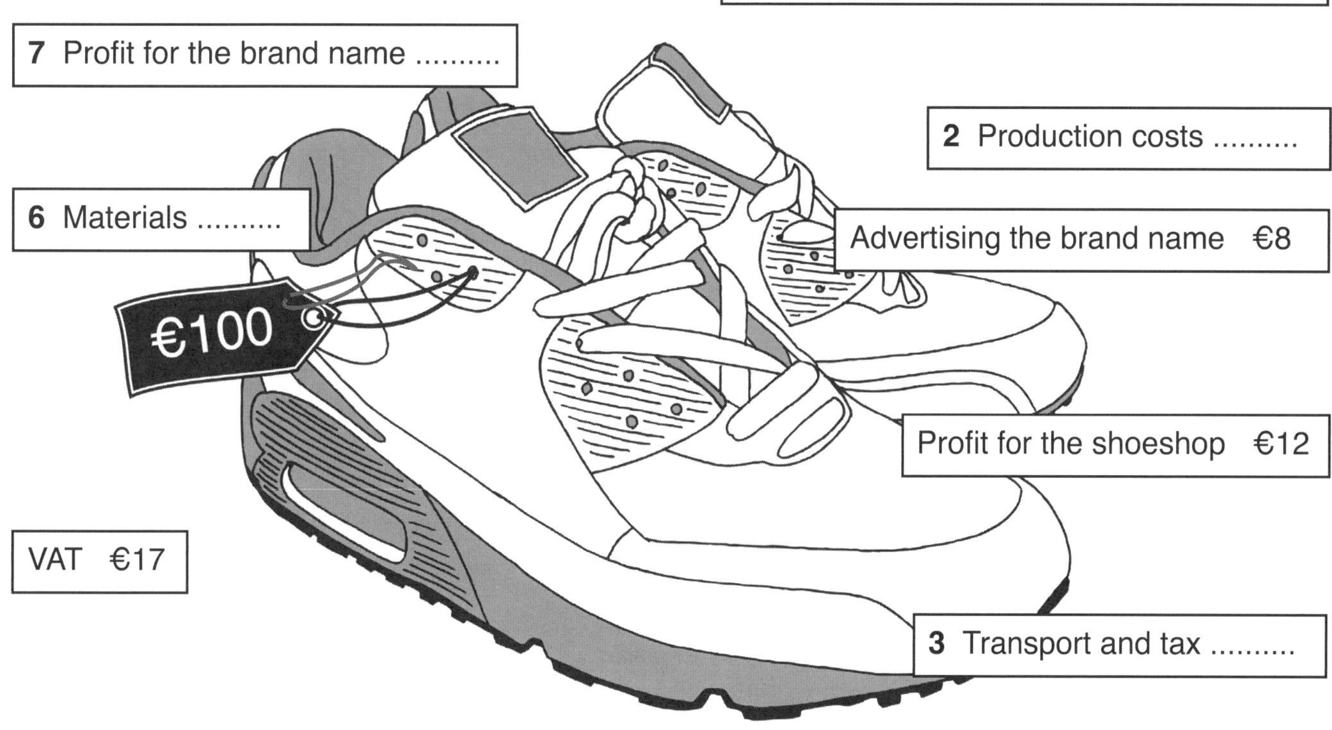

Research into new products €11
1 Wages for the shoemaker's boss ....
7 Profit for the brand name ....
2 Production costs ....
6 Materials ....
Advertising the brand name €8
€100
Profit for the shoeshop €12
VAT €17
3 Transport and tax ....

Rent for the shoe shop €2.50

4 Wages for the shoemaker ....

5 Wages for the shop assistant in the shoe shop ....

---

1 People always want what they don't need.

2 A day in the country or at the beach reminds us that we live in a material world.

3 If you only want what you actually need, you are happy.

4 There is much more to life than having lots of 'things'.

5 Buying things you don't need is just a waste of money.

6 Credit cards make shopping too easy.

Buy Nothing Day

Language focus
tense revision, relative clauses

Key vocabulary
to be bothered, consumerism, credit card, developing countries, to last, natural resources, pittance, to recycle, spending, swap shop

Skills focus
reading: understanding main ideas; speaking: expressing opinions and speculating

Level
upper-intermediate

Time
50 minutes

Preparation
one photocopy, cut up, for each student

Extra notes
If you are interested in finding out more about 'Buy Nothing Day' type it into an Internet search engine.

Warm-up

1. Ask students to copy the questions below in order to carry out a class survey about shopping. If you prefer, ask them to make up all their own questions.
   When did you last go shopping?
   What did you buy?
   How often do you go shopping?
   What do you spend most money on?
   Have you ever bought any clothes that you've never worn?
2. All students stand up and ask six or seven classmates their questions. Then ask some of the students to feed back their findings to the class.

Main activity

1. Write BUY NOTHING DAY on the board and ask students if they've ever heard of it. If they haven't heard about it, don't worry, as they're going to read about it.
2. Give students a copy of the first part of the activity sheet – the article – and ask them to read it quickly just to get the main ideas.
3. Put students into pairs and ask them to share their initial thoughts on Buy Nothing Day.
4. Now put students into groups of four. Tell them you are going to write questions on the board and you want them, in their groups, to talk for two minutes about each question. Write the questions one by one on the board, timing two minutes for each.
   What do you think about the idea of Buy Nothing Day?
   How easy would it be for you to buy absolutely nothing for one day?
   Do you think 'BND' should be changed to Buy Nothing Week? Would you be able to buy nothing for a whole week?
   Do you think it's important to try and consume less? Why / Why not?
5. Ask some of the groups for feedback on what they discussed.
6. Give out the second part of the activity sheet – the headlines – and in the same groups, or in new groups if you prefer, ask students to look at the headlines and to guess what the Buy Nothing Day events are about. If necessary, prompt students by asking questions such as *What do you think happens at this event? What type of people do you think may go to the event?* The headlines are taken from real events.
7. Then compare the ideas of each group and see which group has thought of the most original event or the event that you think is closest to the real event that takes place.

Follow-up

- In small groups, ask students to think of some new events that could take place on Buy Nothing Day that would encourage more young people to get involved. Students could plan the event by deciding where it would take place, who would run it and where they would advertise it, etc. When the groups have finished, ask each group to present their event to the class. You could hold a class vote to choose the most popular event.
- Students design a poster to put up in the classroom or the corridor of your school to raise awareness of Buy Nothing Day.

Buy Nothing Day

Buy Nothing Day started in 1993 and is now an international event that takes place in more than 55 countries around the globe. It is a simple idea to challenge consumer culture and ask people to stop shopping for 24 hours. It takes place on a Saturday at the end of November, when people in many parts of the world have already started thinking about their Christmas shopping.

On Buy Nothing Day people are encouraged to think about what they buy and the possible effects the product may have on the environment and on developing countries. For example, if you buy a new pair of trainers, does it cross your mind to think about where they were made and if the people who made them are treated well by the company? Would it bother you to discover that they were made by workers who were treated badly by their employers and paid a pittance?

According to the organisers of Buy Nothing Day, shopping itself isn't harmful, but what we buy can be. They claim that a mere 20% of the world population consume 80% of the earth's natural resources. They want us, as consumers, to think more about what we buy and to ask ourselves some questions before buying anything new. Here are some of the questions we can put on our check list:

- Do I need it?
- How many do I already have?
- How much will I use it?
- Will it last a long time?
- Could I borrow it from a friend instead of buying my own?
- Is it recyclable?

This year in the UK Buy Nothing Day is on the last Saturday in November. There will be many events in town centres to celebrate the occasion and to encourage shoppers to have a day off and buy absolutely nothing.

The Buy Nothing Day 'Swap Shop'

Community Picnic and Flyer Distribution in the High Street

'SHOPAHOLICS' CLINIC WITH PSYCHOLOGISTS

Second-hand Clothes Fashion Show

Credit card cut-up session

Supermarket Trolley Train

Nervous Nathan's diary

Language focus
past and future simple

Key vocabulary
useful collocations:
to be stressed, to fail an exam, to feel nervous, to have an interview, to introduce a friend, to start a new job, to take a test

Skills focus
reading: extracting key information
speaking: predicting; writing a blog entry

Level
elementary

Time
75 minutes

Preparation
one photocopy for each pair of students

Extra notes
This activity may help to remind us that teenagers too have their worries. If your students are willing to talk about their own lives, there are many opportunities to personalise and extend this lesson.

Warm-up

- Draw a graph on the board, as below, representing a week in the life of a famous person (or your own week). As you plot the lines on the graph, talk about the highs and lows in this person's week (inventing if necessary). Make the events as exciting as possible – you could include award ceremonies, concerts, encounters with the police, break-ups with partners, etc.

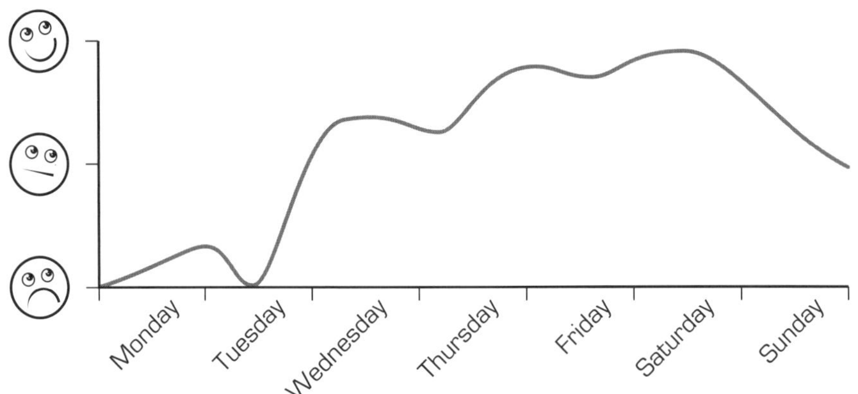
Monday
Tuesday
Wednesday
Thursday
Friday
Saturday
Sunday

Main activity

1. Give out a photocopy to each pair of students and ask them to look at Nathan's diary and to highlight or mark the events of the week that they think will make Nathan feel really nervous. Ask *Which are the most stressful events? Why?*
2. Compare answers and encourage students to expand on the information provided in the diary. For example, they may suggest *I think Nathan will be more nervous on Friday if it's the first time that Sarah has met his Grandma.*
3. Next, ask students to read Nathan's blog – he uses it as an online diary as he finds it helpful to write about his experiences. Ask students to tick the events from the diary that Nathan writes about in the blog.
4. Now, ask students to imagine the rest of Nathan's week. Tell them it's now Sunday and it's time to update the blog. Students work in pairs to write about the rest of Nathan's week. Encourage the students to add in as much additional information as they like.
5. If you think this is too much writing for the time you have available, you could divide the class into four groups – Wednesday, Thursday, Friday and the weekend – and each group just writes about the corresponding day.
6. When the pairs have finished, pass the blogs around the class so students can read each other's work. Ask for some feedback from the class by asking students *Which pair gave Nathan the worst/best week? How does your previous week compare to Nathan's? Was it more or less stressful? Why?*

Follow-up

- If you used the suggested warm-up, now students can draw Nathan's or their own Happy Graph for the previous week.
- Ask students which other situations they consider to be stressful.
- In groups, think of ways that teenagers can avoid feeling nervous and stressed. In groups, ask students to think of their 'Top five tips for staying cool!'

Nervous Nathan's diary

JANUARY 2008

21 Monday

Maths exam

Tennis final with Matt.

22 Tuesday

5pm – Interview – Classic Burger!
Remember to iron shirt.

Homework – Practise English presentation!!!

23 Wednesday

English – presentation of the project!!!
Ahhh!!!

Notes: Buy Gran's birthday present.
Ask Mum for pocket money.
Tell Mum about the detention from Mr Oliver before he phones her.

2008 JANUARY

Thursday 24

Chemistry test
Motorbike driving test

VROOOM!

Homework – physics and geography

Friday 25

Morning break – Mr Oliver's office.
Detention!

I ♥ YOU

Sarah coming to Grandma's birthday party!

Saturday 26

Start job!!! Classic Burger 10am–6pm

Sunday 27

Update blog.

Nervous Nathan's blog

What a week! On Monday I had a really important maths exam. The questions were impossible, and I failed. I felt terrible but Paul failed too and he's really brainy, so then I felt better. Ha-ha! On Monday evening Matt and I lost the final of the tennis tournament. It was bad luck. I had a headache after the exam and didn't play well.

On Tuesday I had an interview to work in Classic Burger on Saturdays. I need the money to buy a new computer. It was awful. I didn't have time to iron my shirt and I was so stressed, I'm sure I was as red as a tomato. But ... I got the job and start this Saturday. I'm already nervous about the first day.

How ambitious are you?

Language focus
questions

Key vocabulary
to achieve, to be (un)ambitious, career, to get what you want, to hurt people's feelings, to lose, to make a difference, self-made millionaire, to win

Skills focus
reading a questionnaire; speaking: agreeing and disagreeing

Level
intermediate

Time
40 minutes

Preparation
one photocopy for each pair or group of 3 students; enough sets of the discussion statements (below teacher's notes), cut up, so each pair or small group will have one statement at a time

Warm-up

1. Dictate the sentences below to your students and ask them to complete it on their own. When you get to the gaps, say *Beep* and ask students to leave a space. Then give them a few minutes to complete the sentence on their own. They can use as many words as they like.
   I think I am ________ *ambitious. My big ambition in life is* ____________.
   For example *I think I am very ambitious. My big ambition in life is to be a film star.*
2. Ask students to read their completed sentences to their neighbour and then ask a few students to volunteer and share their completed sentences with the class.

Main activity

1. Pre-teach any new vocabulary from the maze or make sure students have access to dictionaries.
2. Put students into pairs or threes and give them a copy of the reading maze.
3. Ask students to start where it says 'Start here' and to read the questions and follow their answers through the maze. Encourage them to ask each other occasionally to explain their decisions. You could pre-teach language for reacting to each others' choices such as *Really? Why?* or *No way!* or *Oh yes? Tell me more!*
4. When each student reaches the bottom of the maze and reads their answer, they should discuss in their groups whether or not they agree with it.
5. Now use the discussion statements below. Give each pair or group one statement, then rotate the statements around the groups at two-minute intervals. Tell students they have two minutes to discuss the statement they have. They should say clearly whether or not they agree with it and give reasons why. Encourage students to talk about people they know about who are ambitious, or unambitious, and to use real case scenarios to back up their arguments.

Follow-up

- Students write an interview with a famous person. The questions should include some about ambitions and how ambitious the person is. Students could use the Internet to research the celebrity they choose or they can make up the answers themselves.
- Have a class debate on the subject of *In today's competitive world it's vital to be ambitious.* Divide the class into two groups, 'for' and 'against'.

Discussion statements

✂
Everyone is ambitious, either openly or in secret.
It's good to be ambitious. It helps you reach your goals.
All famous people are ambitious.
People who are very ambitious are often selfish.
The world is becoming more and more competitive.
Unambitious people are often lazy.

11.2 How ambitious are you?

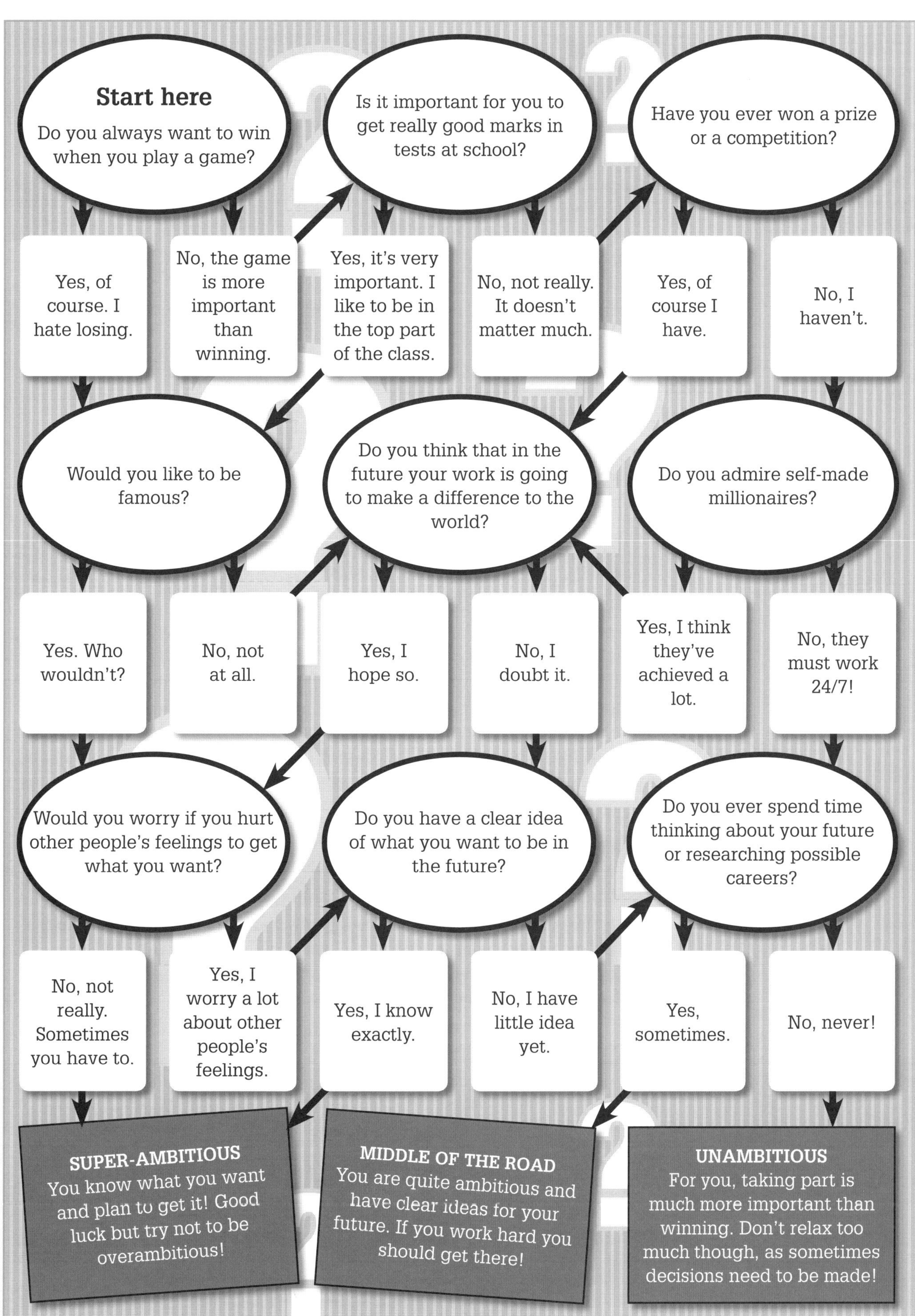

Start here
Do you always want to win when you play a game?
Is it important for you to get really good marks in tests at school?
Have you ever won a prize or a competition?
Yes, of course. I hate losing.
No, the game is more important than winning.
Yes, it's very important. I like to be in the top part of the class.
No, not really. It doesn't matter much.
Yes, of course I have.
No, I haven't.
Would you like to be famous?
Do you think that in the future your work is going to make a difference to the world?
Do you admire self-made millionaires?
Yes. Who wouldn't?
No, not at all.
Yes, I hope so.
No, I doubt it.
Yes, I think they've achieved a lot.
No, they must work 24/7!
Would you worry if you hurt other people's feelings to get what you want?
Do you have a clear idea of what you want to be in the future?
Do you ever spend time thinking about your future or researching possible careers?
No, not really. Sometimes you have to.
Yes, I worry a lot about other people's feelings.
Yes, I know exactly.
No, I have little idea yet.
Yes, sometimes.
No, never!
SUPER-AMBITIOUS
You know what you want and plan to get it! Good luck but try not to be overambitious!
MIDDLE OF THE ROAD
You are quite ambitious and have clear ideas for your future. If you work hard you should get there!
UNAMBITIOUS
For you, taking part is much more important than winning. Don't relax too much though, as sometimes decisions need to be made!

Thinking time

Language focus
future tenses, present simple

Key vocabulary
ambition, promise, worry

Skills focus
speaking and writing: sharing information

Level
upper-intermediate

Time
40 minutes

Preparation
one photocopy, cut in half, for every 2 students

Extra notes
This activity will work best in a calm and supportive atmosphere where students feel able to talk openly about their feelings. However, students needn't feel forced into expressing their worries and dreams. Usually students, like teachers, only reveal as much personal information as they choose to and this should be respected throughout the lesson. During the activity students need some quiet thinking time. You could put on some relaxing music in the background.

Warm-up

- Play a game of Hangman to elicit the following words: *worry, promise, hope, dream.* As each word is discovered, put it in a cloud on the board and ask students what words they think of when they think about each word.

Main activity

1. Give half an activity sheet to each student (the two halves are identical) and set a time limit for students to complete it. If you think your students may need some prompting, model the activity first by putting some examples of your own in the gaps. For example:

   Me:
   A personal ambition: *To write a novel before I'm forty.*
   A hope for the future: *I hope I will pass my driving test next month.*
   A worry: *I spend too much time at work and not enough time at home.*
   A dream: *To travel around Thailand.*

   By sharing your own worries and dreams with your students you will give the students a chance to see you as a real person rather than just their English teacher. They will probably want to ask you questions to find out more, so if you are comfortable with this, encourage them to do so.
2. Put students into small groups to share their thoughts and ideas from their activity sheets. It may be a good idea for students to choose the groups themselves, so they are working with classmates they like, trust and respect.
3. If appropriate for your class, ask for some whole-class feedback on what they learnt about one another. If you want to keep the activity more private, ask students to write about what they talked about.

Follow-up

- Ask students to choose one of the categories: Me, The planet, My friends and family, or My city and country and to develop their thoughts in a composition. Offer guidance on how to structure the writing if necessary.
- If you have students who are musically inclined, ask them to work in small groups and to put their thoughts from the activity into the lyrics of a song. They could choose a well known or popular song with a catchy tune to sing it to. If your students prefer, they could write a poem instead of song lyrics.

11.3 Thinking time

Me	The planet	My friends and family	My city or country
■ A personal ambition:	■ A hope for the future:	■ A hope for the future:	■ A hope for the future:
■ A hope for the future:	■ A worry:	■ A worry:	■ A promise:
■ A worry:	■ A personal promise:	■ A dream:	■ A worry:
■ A dream:	■ A dream:	■ A promise for my friends or family:	■ A dream:

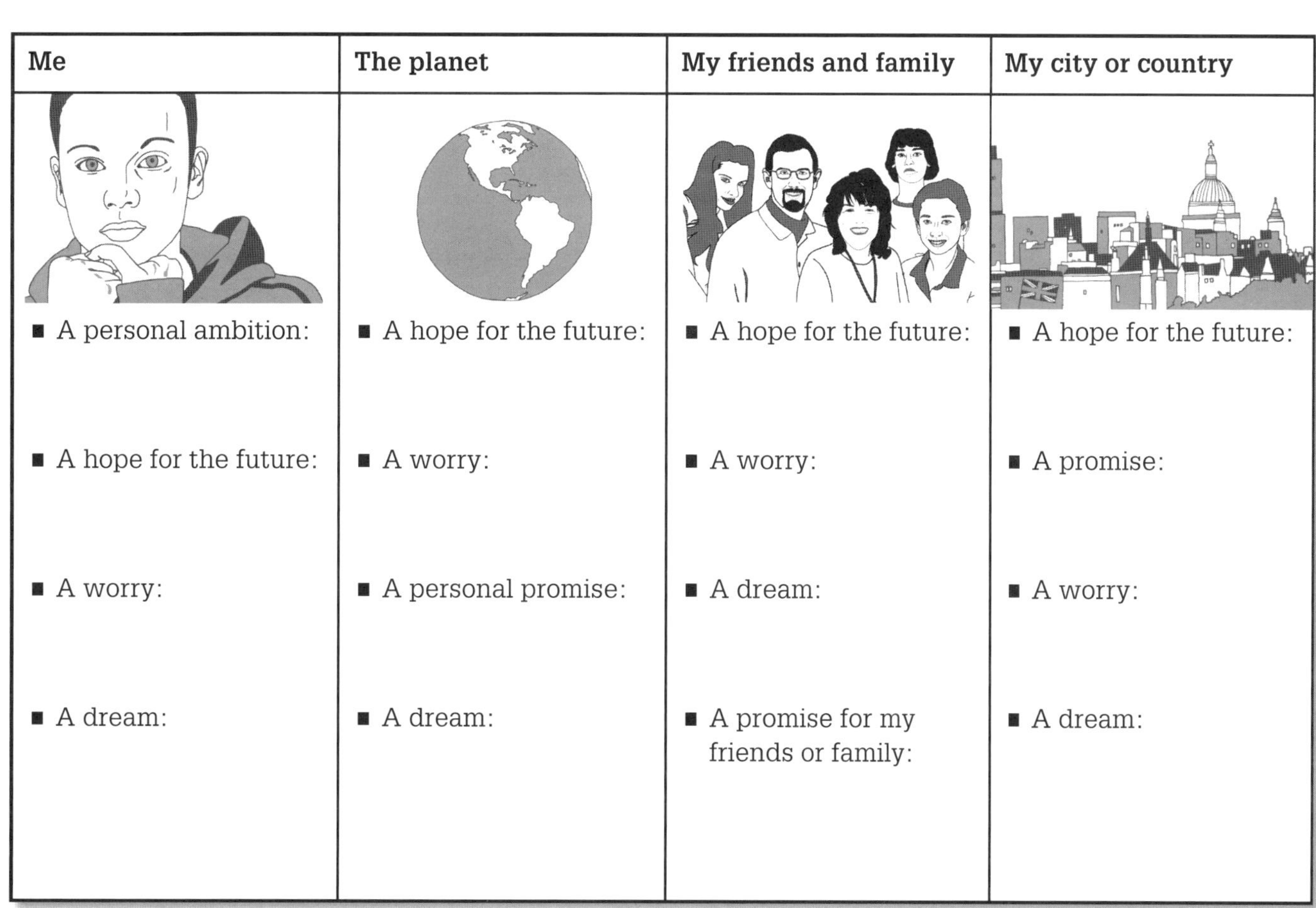

Me	The planet	My friends and family	My city or country
■ A personal ambition:	■ A hope for the future:	■ A hope for the future:	■ A hope for the future:
■ A hope for the future:	■ A worry:	■ A worry:	■ A promise:
■ A worry:	■ A personal promise:	■ A dream:	■ A worry:
■ A dream:	■ A dream:	■ A promise for my friends or family:	■ A dream:

Newsite

Language focus
present simple, present continuous, *going to*, past simple, future simple

Key vocabulary
celebrity, destroy, destruction, emergency services, headline, hurricane, international, local, nature, news, science

Skills focus
reading: understanding main ideas; writing: news reports

Level
elementary

Time
60 minutes +

Preparation
one photocopy for each student

Warm-up

- Ask your students some of the following questions:
  Is it important to know what's happening in the news?
  Do you ever read newspapers? If so, which ones?
  Do you think newspapers will exist in ten years' time?
  Do you ever read news on the Internet?
  Are there any good TV news programmes or news web pages for people your age? If so, what are they? If not, do you think it's a good idea to have news programmes and websites specifically for young people?

Main activity

1. Give out an activity sheet to each student and ask them to read the stories on the news web page very quickly. They should only skim read at this stage.
2. Then ask students to choose the correct headline to go with each story and write it on the dotted line.
3. Now, ask students to read the news stories in detail. They can read them in any order, as you would a newspaper or a website. Tell them you don't expect them to understand every word; encourage them to read for general understanding. They can use the pictures to help them too.
4. Ask students which articles they chose to read first and last, and ask them why. To check general understanding, ask all the students to think of one question related to one of the articles they read. They should write this question down. Then ask several of the students to ask their questions to the whole class.
5. Now tell students they are going to make their own news web page for teenagers. The activity sheet can be used as a model. Put students into groups of between three and six. They should work together to produce six short articles – one for each of the main sections. If you have a mixed-ability class, think carefully about whether you want to group students in friendship groups, mixed groups of weak and strong students or group similar levels together.
6. If you have Internet access or access to newspapers and magazines, these can be used as sources for the stories. If not, students should use their imaginations or use news stories they've heard recently.
7. When the groups have finished, they should stick the separate articles together to make the web page. (If you have computer access, you could make a more professional version.)
8. Display all the students' work and encourage students to read each others' web pages and prepare questions about the stories they've read.

Follow-up

- Use the stories that students have created to make a radio news programme. Record the students reading out their stories. If you have a camera, you could make a news programme by setting up a news studio and filming the stories being read out.
- Give some students the role of journalists and others the roles of people from the news stories they've written. The journalists should interview the people in the news stories. You will need to give time and support for students to prepare the questions and answers. This could be filmed too if you have a camera. If not, each group could perform their interview in front of the class.

12.1 Newsite

Graham Surfs to World Championship

WORLD CUP FEVER HITS THE STREETS

Lola Aston becomes a Mum

Today's Forecast

World News

....

Hurricane Molly is causing destruction in Mexico and the eye of the storm is currently moving north towards the USA. Yesterday, thousands of people lost their homes as the storm destroyed everything in its path. Emergency services are travelling to the affected areas to help.

Local News

....

Local boy Graham Holey, aged 14, is going to represent the UK in the World Surf Championships this summer. The competition will take place in Hawaii on July 18th. Graham hopes to bring back a medal, but he knows it will be difficult to win. "The best surfers in the world will be there and it's going to be tough, but I'll do my best. Surfing's my life!" said Graham when we interviewed him at his school yesterday.

Celebrity News

....

Pop star Lola Aston had a baby girl! Yesterday evening pop star Lola Aston, age 23, gave birth to her first baby and named her Moonshine Grace. Her boyfriend is from the group The Buzz and both father and mother are happy and well.

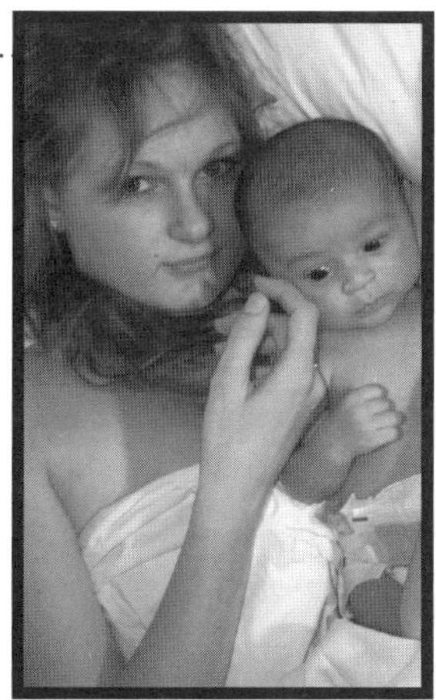

Sports

....

The football World Cup starts next week. As always, it's going to be an exciting competition. 'World Cup Fever' is starting to hit the streets of England, as flags appear in the windows of houses and cars. Do England really have a chance? We want to know what you think. Vote here:

YES! NO!

Science and Nature

....

An extremely rare type of parrot from the Bird of Paradise Park in Hayle, Cornwall, was saved by local dentist Philip Bubble. The parrot, one of only six of its type in the UK, has a rare disease and her beak was weak and broken, meaning the parrot couldn't eat. Mr Bubble made a false beak for the parrot and now she can eat again. Workers at the park are happy with her progress and hope to find some eggs in her cage soon.

The Weather

....

Today will be mainly cloudy with rain showers in the north of the country. In the south it will be cloudy with some sunny periods. Maximum temperatures will be 17°C and minimum temperatures will be 9°C.

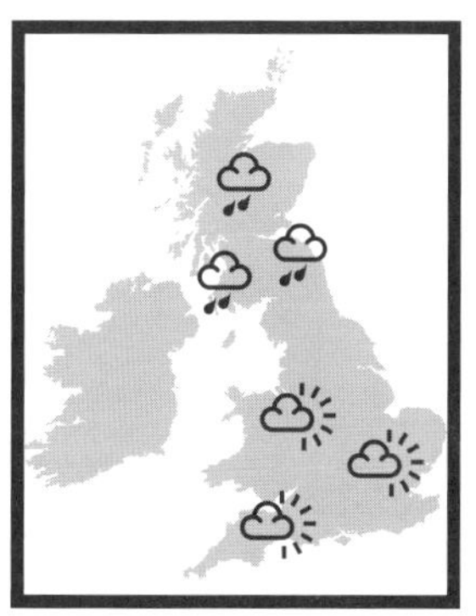

HURRICANE MOLLY DESTROYS HOMES

Rare Parrot saved by Dentist

Paparazzi pyramid

Language focus
giving opinions

Key vocabulary
celebrity, gossip, journalist, media, paparazzi, visual image

Skills focus
speaking: agreeing and disagreeing, fluency

Level
intermediate

Time
40 minutes

Preparation
one photocopy, cut up, for each pair of students; a selection of photos from newspapers and magazines (see Warm-up)

Warm-up

1. Cut out a wide selection of very different photographs from newspapers and magazines and stick them around the room. Ask students to wander around and look at the photos and talk to other students about these questions:
   What do you know about the situation/place/people in the picture?
   Do you think any of the photos shouldn't have been published? Why / Why not?
2. Afterwards, ask them which photo was most memorable and why.

Main activity

1. Pre-teach any new vocabulary from the activity sheet.
2. Put students into pairs and give each pair a set of discussion statements. You may want to consider pairing stronger students with weaker students. Ask them to read the statements one by one and to make sure they understand them. Ask students to think individually first of all about whether or not they agree with each statement.
3. When the individuals have had some quiet thinking time they should speak to their partner and discuss reasons behind their decision to agree or disagree with each statement. The pair can agree to disagree, but they should try and persuade their partner to see their point of view. As the pairs do this, they will start to formulate their opinions as well as listening to their partner's view. The pair should put the statements in three piles on the table: Agree / Not sure / Disagree. This stage should take a maximum of ten minutes. They will have time to develop their ideas later.
4. When two pairs have finished, put them together to make a group of four. They should now compare which statements they put in each pile and discuss their differences.
5. If you have a big class, continue the pyramid discussion and put two groups of four together to make a group of eight. If your group isn't large enough to do this, ask the whole class for some feedback from their discussions.
6. As students do this activity it gives you a perfect opportunity to monitor their speaking. The focus should be on fluency, but you may want to take note of the mistakes you hear, in order to use them later on in an error correction slot. As you are monitoring them, feed in any new language they may need. If you like, join in the group discussions from time to time and try to go against the general opinion of the group occasionally in order to provoke discussion.

Follow-up

- Use the discussion statements again but this time give out YOU TOTALLY AGREE or YOU COMPLETELY DISAGREE cards to certain students so they have to argue against their real opinion.
- Record a few minutes of a local TV news programme. Watch it with the sound off and ask your students to tell you about the news stories. If they don't usually watch the news and have no idea what the stories are about, put them in groups to guess and make up the story that goes with the pictures.
- If celebrity gossip magazines are popular where you work, bring some in to the class and then ask students to invent a story about a famous celebrity for one of these magazines. It could be as ridiculous as they like.

12.2 Paparazzi pyramid

You can't believe everything you read in the newspapers.

People are only interested in bad news.

Famous people shouldn't complain when the paparazzi take their photographs.

Some strong images on the news invade people's privacy.

Visual images are essential to understand what is happening in the world.

The world is getting smaller as news is travelling faster.

In ten years' time newspapers won't exist.

Bad news travels faster than good news.

A photograph speaks a thousand words.

Journalists and photographers do a very important job.

TV news competition

Language focus
language of news broadcasts

Key vocabulary
language chunks from news programmes: *Good evening and welcome to … ; Firstly, … ; And now to … , where … ; And finally, … ; That's all from me for tonight, so …*

Skills focus
speaking: presenting information

Level
upper-intermediate

Time
75 minutes +

Preparation
one photocopy for each group of 4 or 5 students

Warm-up

- Ask students how important they think it is to know about what is going on in the world. Then read these statements and ask students to stand up if they agree with them. Alternatively, dictate the statements and ask pairs to discuss them briefly.
  Watching the news on TV is boring.
  It's important to know what's happening in the world.
  Local news is more interesting than international news.
  There are some really good news programmes on TV for people our age.

Main activity

1. Ask students a few more questions about the final statement in the warm-up task. Localise and personalise the questions. For example, if there are any news programmes for teens in your country, what do the students think about them? If there aren't any, do they think that a programme specifically aimed at young people would be a good idea?
2. Tell students that they're going to take part in a competition and make a news programme. Put students into groups of four or five and give each group a copy of the poster to read.
3. Tell students that part of the challenge for this activity is to see how they work together as a group. Make it clear that you will be observing their teamwork as well as assessing the final product.
4. Set a time limit for completion of the whole task and let students work together to prepare their TV programme.
5. If you would like them to use real news stories, provide a selection of newspapers and magazines, or allow them to access the Internet.
6. Feed in any useful language your students may be lacking, but remember the target audience is young people, so encourage your students to explain the news items in a friendly and informal way.
7. If you have access to a camera, film the programmes and watch them back as a class. If you only have a voice recorder, you may decide to make the programme into a radio show. If you don't have any equipment to record the students' work, have a live showing of the programmes.
8. When all the groups have presented their programme, hold a class vote to see who wins the prizes.

Follow-up

- If time permits, extend the activity over two classes. Students can make props for their show and bring in special clothes to wear for the recording.
- Ask students to find a funny or strange news story in a paper or on the Internet. They then explain the story to their group or to the whole class.

12.3 TV news competition

bubble

Production Company

Bubble Production Company is looking for a team of young people who think they've got what it takes to make a fresh and dynamic news programme for young people.

Prizes

1st prize – A two-week holiday in Australia for all the team

2nd prize – Reporters' technical pack for all the team including a laptop, a digital voice recorder and a digital camera

3rd prize – Flat-screen top-of-the-range televisions for all the team

Are you up for the challenge? If so, here are the requirements:

- The programme needs a name and a logo.
- It should last for four or five minutes and contain at least three of the following sections: international news, local news, sports, weather, celebrity news, music news, environmental news or weird science.
- You can use real or invented news stories.
- The programme must appeal to young people aged 13–20.

What are you waiting for? Rise to the challenge! For more information check out our website www.bubbleproductionco.com

Family match

Language focus
questions and answers in the present simple; family relationships; possessive *'s*

Key vocabulary
extended family vocabulary including: *aunty, daughter, grandma, half-brother, half-sister, mother-in-law, nephew, relations, second husband, sister-in-law, son, step-dad, step-daughter*

Skills focus
speaking: asking and answering questions

Level
elementary

Time
40 minutes

Preparation
one photocopy, cut up, for every 16 students. If you have a small group, remove one of the family sets or give some students two cards each.

Extra notes
This activity is designed to extend students' knowledge of family vocabulary so they can talk about their own and others' actual families, which often include step-relations and half-brothers and sisters.

Warm-up

1. Draw your own family tree on the board. If you have any photos of your family, you could show these as you introduce them. Students will probably be really interested to see photos of your relatives. As you introduce the various members, write their names on the board.
2. Ask your class some simple questions about who's who to elicit the family vocabulary.
3. Then give students some sentence beginnings to complete, for example: *Rachel and Clare are* ... (Joanna's sisters). If the possessive *'s* is new to your students, now is the time to highlight it and ensure understanding of its use.

Main activity

1. Revise the necessary questions for this activity by asking some of your students the following questions and writing them on the board if necessary.
   Who do you live with?
   Have you got any brothers or sisters?
   Do you live in a house or a flat?
2. Give each student one of the family cards. Keep the cards in family sets by removing a family set if you only have twelve students or by giving some students two cards if you don't have a number that's divisible by four.
3. Tell them that they must not show anyone else their card. They should read it and can refer to it if necessary, but they mustn't let anyone else read it.
4. Students then walk around asking each other questions until they find the other three members of their family. When students find their families, tell them they must introduce one another so they know as much as possible about each of their relations.
5. When students have had time to get to know their new families, ask each student to introduce one other member of their family, for example: *This is my Dad. He's called Romesh and he loves cooking.* (Hari)
6. Then, in their family groups, ask the students to draw a family tree of their new family. They can invent any missing information and elaborate on the details given to them on the cards. Each group then presents their family tree to the class.

Follow-up

- Students stay in their new 'family groups' from the activity to create a role play. Imagine a typical family scenario, like preparing a meal or all watching television together, and students write a simple dialogue to depict the scene.
- Students make their own family tree posters to display on the wall. If possible, they could bring in photos to illustrate them.

13.1 Family match

The Batras

Romesh

You live with your wife, your mother-in-law and your son. Your son is a student; he wants to be a vet. You love cooking and experimenting with new dishes.

Sarah

You live with your husband, your mother and your son. You love gardening and you spend hours in your garden at home.

Betsy

You live with your daughter, your son-in-law and your very clever grandson. Your son-in-law is a great cook. You love reading books in the garden.

Hari

You are an only child. You live with your parents and your grandma. You are a student and you love animals. Your dad is the main cook in your house.

The Plaths

Tom

You live with your partner, your son and your sister, who's living with you for a few months because she's just separated from her husband. You live in a small flat in the town centre.

Silvia

You live with your partner and your son. Your sister-in-law is also staying with you for a while. She helps to babysit for your son sometimes, but there's not really enough space in your apartment.

Marc

You live with your parents and your aunty. You love having your aunty at home with you too. She's good fun! You hope she's going to stay forever.

Helen

You're living with your brother and his family for a while. You've just separated from your husband. You like playing with your favourite nephew. You like living in the centre of town.

The Needhams

Clare

You live with your two children and your second husband. You and your husband work together; you are both doctors in the local hospital. You live in a big house.

Patrick

You live with your wife, your son and your step-daughter. You met your wife at work, in the hospital. You love your job but you hate working at night.

Agatha

You live with your mum, your step-dad, and your half-brother. When you're ill your mum and step-dad always know what to do. Your half-brother is younger than you and you like playing tennis together.

Oliver

You live with your parents and your older half-sister. You love football but sometimes you play tennis too. Your half-sister isn't bad at tennis. Your parents work really hard, sometimes at night time too.

The Clarkes

Nicola

You live with your three children. You live in a big flat in the centre of the city. You are a teacher at the local school. You love going swimming and going to the cinema.

Lola

You live with your mum, your sister and your brother. You sometimes see your mum when you're at school. You go swimming every week with your mum.

Frankie

You live with your two sisters and your mum. You are the baby of the family. You like playing games with your sisters and going swimming with your mum.

Jasmine

You live with your mum, your sister and your little brother. You live in a large flat in the city centre. You see your mum at home and at school and you love going to the cinema with her.

In your parents' shoes

Language focus
past simple, past continuous, language of reason and persuasion: *in order to … ; so as to … ; Go on, please let me … ; I promise I'll …*

Key vocabulary
words to talk about typical teenage scenarios and dilemmas

Skills focus
speaking: explaining, persuading

Level
intermediate

Time
50 minutes

Preparation
one photocopy, cut up, for every 4 students

Extra notes
This activity may well lead to some interesting discussions about the difficulties of being a teenager, and it will also give the students a chance to see things from their parents' point of view.

Warm-up

1. Draw two circles on the board. Write in one circle the word PARENTS and in the other the word TEENAGERS. Ask students what comes to mind when they read these words and write their ideas in the circles. Students could do this individually at first or you could do it as a whole-class activity.
2. When the circles are full of their ideas, ask students if they think being a parent is a difficult job. Why / Why not? Students should try and support their ideas with reasons. If you like, ask students if being a teenager is difficult.

Main activity

1. Divide the class into two groups. All the students in one group are going to take the role of Parents and all the students in the other group are going to take the role of Teenagers. If you have an odd number, have an extra Parent rather than an extra Teenager and they can work in a 'mum and dad' pair. In fact, if you have any particularly weak students you may decide to pair them with a stronger student to make a 'mum and dad' pair.
2. Within the Parents group, divide the group into four smaller groups and give each member of each smaller group the same Parents role card. Do the same with the group of Teenagers: divide it into four smaller groups and give each group member the same role card. Keep the blank cards for later.
3. Give students time in these groups to gather ideas and think about language they will use during the role-play. The Parents should use their imagination to think of more details about the day they've had and the Teenagers can start to plan what they are going to say to offer a convincing argument to their parents. At this stage, monitor the groups carefully and offer ideas. Feed in any new language that students may need.
4. Now, pair up the Parents and the Teenagers. Put one group of Parents with one group of Teenagers and pair them off. Give the pair time to do the role-play. Encourage them to run through it several times. Decide if you want them to write out the dialogue or, if you prefer, to keep it more spontaneous.
5. If your students enjoy the activity, why not ask a few of the pairs to demonstrate their role-play to the whole class.
6. Then change the roles. The Parents now become Teenagers and vice versa.
7. Now, discuss with your students how they felt being in their parents' shoes. If your students are mature enough, you could ask them whether they would like to become parents one day and if they think they will be good parents or not.
8. Finally, give each pair of students a blank Teenager or Parent card and ask them to write the role cards. They could base them on real-life situations or make them up. They can exaggerate the situations and the way the Parents are feeling. Collect the role cards in and save them to use in a future class.

Follow-up

- Do the role-plays using the role cards created by your students.
- Students think about the best and worst aspects of being parents and/or teenagers. Groups draw up a list and then compare with other groups' ideas.
- Students write a fun list of 'Top Tips for being a Good Teenager' or 'Top Tips for being a Cool Parent'.

13.2 In your parents' shoes

Teenagers

You went out with your friends and were supposed to be back by 11 pm. However, you were having such a good time that you didn't realise the time. It's 11.45 pm when you arrive home. Your parents are waiting for you. Try to convince them that you are late for a good reason.	You stayed in all last weekend to study for your final exams but in fact you spent all weekend in your room on the computer, playing games and chatting to friends. Your parents thought you were studying. Now you have failed two of your final exams and have to tell your parents.
You really want to go to a concert next month as your favourite group is coming to town. The tickets for the concert are very expensive and it will take place on a school night. Try to convince your parents to let you go, and to give you some money to help pay for the ticket.	Next weekend your parents want to take you to visit your grandmother, who lives quite far away. There's nothing to do in her village and you usually get bored. Next weekend is also your best friend's birthday party and you really want to go. Try to convince your parents to let you stay at home (or at your best friend's house) instead of going to visit your grandmother.
Write your own teenager situation here: ______	Write your own teenager situation here: ______

Parents

You're really tired. You've had a terrible day at work.	You're in a good mood today. You had some good news at work.	You're in a bad mood. The traffic on the way home was awful and you're tired and hungry.
You're in a real hurry. You have to be at work in 15 minutes.	Write your own parent situation here: ______	Write your own parent situation here: ______

A problem shared ...

Language focus
giving advice – modal verbs: *should, would*

Key vocabulary
verbs + prepositions: *to argue with, to be addicted to, to be stressed out, to complain about, to get in trouble, to go mad, to pick on somebody, to see eye to eye with somebody, to worry about*

Skills focus
speaking: asking for and giving advice, focusing on accuracy and good intonation

Level
upper-intermediate

Time
40 minutes

Preparation
one photocopy, cut up, for each pair or group of 3. Pairs should get a copy of Dialogue 1 and groups of 3 a copy of Dialogue 2

Warm-up

1. Put your students into small groups and ask them to think of some typical problems that teenagers face.
2. Ask each group to read out their top five problems and see if the groups had similar ideas. Write a list of the top five most common problems. Ask your students how good they are at giving advice to their friends when they have problems.

Main activity

1. Elicit language that is useful for giving advice, for example *If I were you, I'd* + infinitive, *How about* + *-ing?*, *Why don't you* + infinitive?, *I think you should* + infinitive. Practise saying the phrases aloud.
2. Put students into pairs or groups of three. Tell them they are going to work with a dialogue. They are going to be given the skeleton of the dialogue and they have to create the rest. Tell them at this stage that, as they have a lot of help with the dialogue, you expect them to be very accurate with their language and also to think about their pronunciation, especially their intonation. Give some examples of good intonation for offering advice.
3. Give the students the appropriate dialogue – Dialogue 1 for pairs and Dialogue 2 for groups of three. Ask for a volunteer in each group to be 'A' and give them a problem card.
4. Give students time to go through the dialogue, develop it and practise their roles. As they're practising, monitor carefully and offer advice on how they could make their dialogue sound as natural as possible. However, even though you are focusing on accuracy, don't attempt to correct every mistake you hear as you are monitoring. You could subtly take notes of the common errors during the activity and work with them afterwards.
5. If you have access to a voice recorder, this would be a good activity to record and listen back to; if not, you could ask a few groups to perform their dialogue in front of the class.
6. Mix up the groups, and this time, change the students who take the role of 'A'.

Follow-up

- Ask each student to write one problem on a slip of paper. If you like, you could ask your students to write ridiculous, joke problems which would make for some funny dialogues. Collect all the problems in, redistribute them to different students, and ask students to do the dialogues again, with or without the scripts to guide them.
- Repeat the dialogues without the scripts and this time the 'listeners' (Bs and Cs) are going to be really bad at listening to problems and giving advice. They could be in a real hurry, be impatient and give terrible advice to the student with the problem.

13.3 A problem shared ...

Dialogue 1 – Pairs

A: Hi, ________ . Have you got five minutes?

B: Yeah, what's up?

A: Well, I've got a bit of a problem.

B: Go on. A problem shared is a problem halved!

A: [EXPLAIN THE PROBLEM]

B: [REACT TO THE PROBLEM + ASK FOR MORE DETAILS]

A: [GIVE MORE DETAILS]

B: [REACT TO THE INFORMATION]

A: So, what do you think I should do?

B: Well, if I were you I'd … [GIVE SOME ADVICE]

A: [REACT TO ADVICE]

B: [REPLY]

A: [THANK YOUR FRIEND + END THE CONVERSATION NATURALLY]

Dialogue 2 – Groups of three

A: Hello, I'm glad to see you two.

B: Hi, ________ .

C: Hello ________ . Are you alright? You look a bit upset. What's up?

A: There *is* something I'm worried about, actually.

B: Come on then, tell us all about it.

C: You never know, we may be able to help.

A: OK, well … [EXPLAIN THE PROBLEM]

B + C: [REACT TO THE PROBLEM + ASK FOR MORE DETAILS]

A: [GIVE MORE DETAILS]

B: Well, if I were you I'd … [GIVE SOME ADVICE]

C: Yeah, or how about …? [GIVE SOME ADVICE]

A: [REACT TO ADVICE]

B + C: [REPLY]

A: [THANK YOUR FRIENDS + END THE CONVERSATION NATURALLY]

Problem cards

One of your friends is copying your style: your hair, your clothes, your accessories, and you're fed up. It's getting to the point of being embarrassing!

You're not getting on at all well with your parents. You don't see eye to eye on anything these days and you're always arguing.

You think one of your teachers is picking on you. You don't like the subject but you do most of the work. Even so, it's always you that gets in trouble in the class.

One of your friends is addicted to Internet chat rooms. You're worried about them as they seem to be meeting strange people and now they send text messages all day too to these new cyber 'friends'.

One of your best friends used to be lots of fun, but now they spend all day playing on the computer. You're worried about them. They'd much prefer to stay in all weekend than to go out with you and your mates.

You want to drastically change your image but your parents don't want you to. You'd really like to have a piercing, a tattoo or a crazy hair style but you know your parents would go mad.

You are worried about a friend of yours who is on a very strict diet to lose weight. They hardly eat anything now and you're sure they have a problem.

You're sure your sister/brother is your parents' favourite. They always say how fantastic they are and they only seem to complain about you: your exam results, your friends, etc.

You are stressed out with school work and don't have time to do the things you really want to do. You have four exams next week and three projects to finish and you just don't know where to begin.

Square eyes

Language focus
question words (*wh*-questions and *how much* / *how many*), present simple, past simple

Key vocabulary
actor, actress, favourite, how many, how much, popcorn, TV presenter, what, when, which, who
types of film, e.g. *comedy, romantic, science fiction, thriller*

Skills focus
speaking: asking and answering questions
writing: note taking

Level
elementary

Time
45 minutes

Preparation
one photocopy, cut up, for each pair of students

Extra notes
This activity will give you the chance to find out about your students' viewing habits, favourite films and TV programmes, actors and actresses, etc. You could use this knowledge to plan further activities connected to your students' interests in this area.

Warm-up

1. Draw a simple table on the board with two columns and two rows. Above the table, label one column TELEVISION and the other CINEMA. Label the top row ADVANTAGES and the bottom row DISADVANTAGES.
2. Put students into small groups and ask them to think about the advantages and disadvantages of TV and cinema, and to fill in the table with their ideas. Then gather some group feedback from the whole class.

Main activity

1. Tell your students they're going to do a questionnaire to find out who in the class has 'square eyes', meaning that they watch a lot of TV or films.
2. Put students into pairs and give one student in each pair the television questions and the other student the cinema questions. Ask the students to read the questions carefully and complete them with the question words on the left. Then all the students should write two questions of their own for numbers 7 and 8.

> Answers
> *Television questions*
> **1** How much **2** When **3** What **4** Who **5** Which **6** How many
> *Cinema questions*
> **1** When **2** What **3** Who **4** How much **5** How many **6** What

3. Then students carry out the questionnaire in their pairs. Draw their attention to the speech bubble that reads 'And you?' When students get an answer to their question, the student answering should ask their partner 'And you?' so they answer the same question. Students should make notes of their partner's replies.
4. When the pairs have finished, they should be able to give a summary of the results of their questionnaire. This could be either oral or written.

Follow-up

- Prepare a lesson using a recording of your students' favourite TV programme or film. You could bring in a clip and play it without the sound. Ask your students to imagine the dialogue. Choose a two-minute sequence and your students can act as 'dubbers' to dub the sequence into English.
- Bring in some TV guides or information about what's on at the local cinema. Ask students to choose their TV viewing for the night, or to pick a film they would all like to go and see. They should be encouraged to justify their choices.

14.1 Square eyes

Television questions

Who
How much
What
Which
How many
When

And you?

1 ______________ television do you watch in a normal week?

2 ______________ do you watch TV?

3 ______________ did you watch on TV yesterday?

4 ______________ is your favourite TV presenter?

5 ______________ are your favourite TV programmes?

6 ______________ hours of TV did you watch yesterday?

7 ____?

8 ____?

Cinema questions

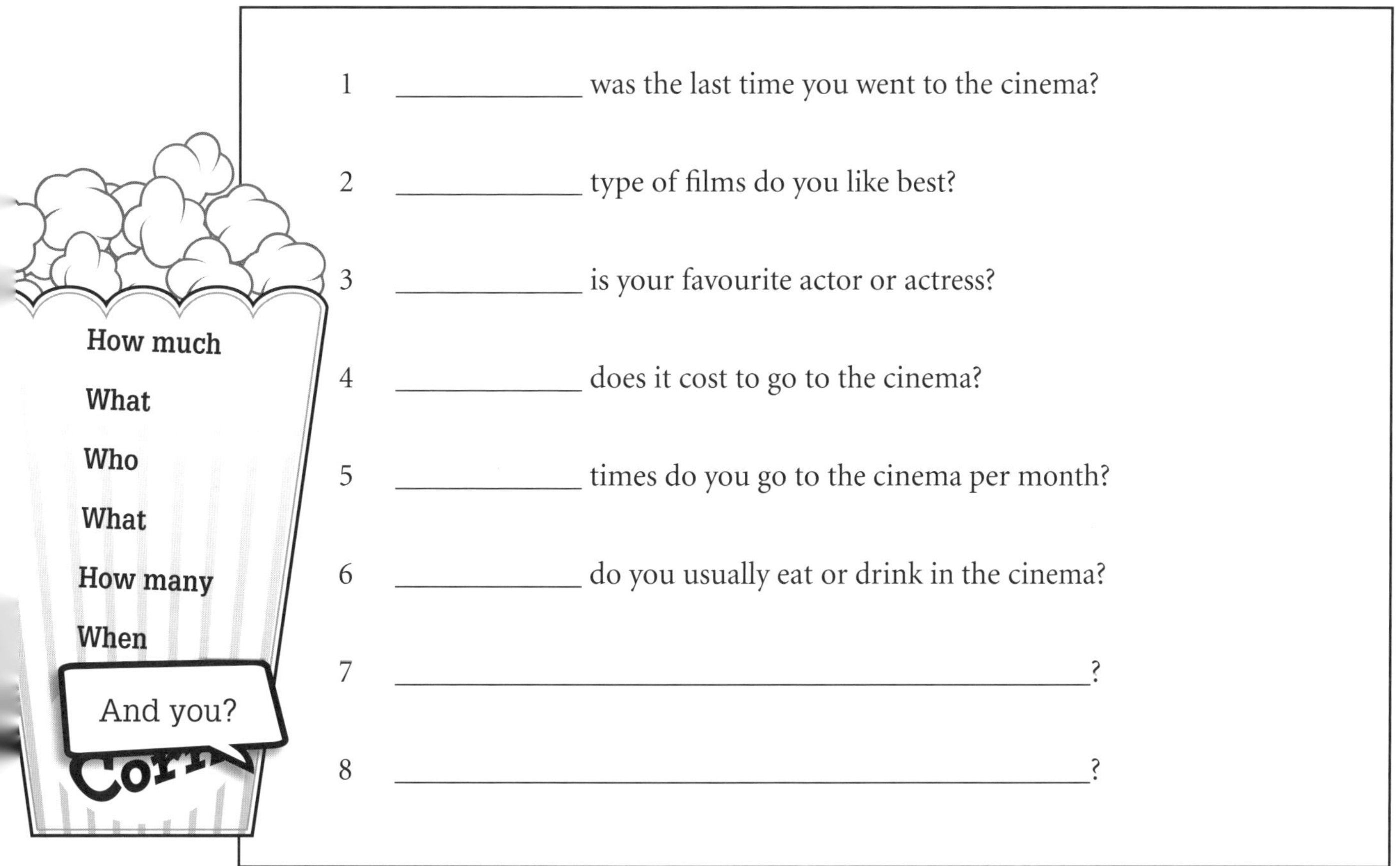
How much
What
Who
What
How many
When
And you?

1 ______________ was the last time you went to the cinema?

2 ______________ type of films do you like best?

3 ______________ is your favourite actor or actress?

4 ______________ does it cost to go to the cinema?

5 ______________ times do you go to the cinema per month?

6 ______________ do you usually eat or drink in the cinema?

7 ____?

8 ____?

Murder of the movie maker

Language focus
present simple and present continuous to explain the plot of a film

Key vocabulary
film genres: *action, adventure, detective, documentary, drama, historical, horror, romantic comedy, science fiction, thriller*
language for horror films: *to be set, blood, cast, character, dialogue, horrific, location, motive, murder weapon, opening scene, plot, scream, spooky, vampire*

Skills focus
speaking: planning and making suggestions; writing a movie dialogue

Level
intermediate

Time
45 minutes

Preparation
one photocopy for each pair or group of 3

Extra notes
This activity would also work well as an individual writing task.

Warm-up

- Ask your students what films they have watched recently. When they tell you, go on to ask them what type of film they were. As they tell you the different film genres, write them up on the board. If some are missing, ask the students simple questions to elicit the following types, then ask them which are their favourites: *action, adventure, detective, documentary, drama, historical, horror, romantic comedy, science fiction, thriller.*

Main activity

1. Before you begin this activity you have to tell your class a little story. Try to make it as believable as possible by telling the class that you read it in the paper yesterday or saw it on the news. Add as much extra information as you like by embellishing the story.
   A famous film writer was working on a new horror film which was going to be a best-selling Hollywood blockbuster, like all his other films. He had just begun to plan the movie when a horrific event took place. A masked man broke into his house, went into his office, where he was working, and killed him!
2. At this stage ask students to imagine who it may have been and what the motive of the murder could have been. They may suggest it was a rival movie maker, or an actor who hadn't been chosen for a part in a film. Let students speculate. Then continue the tale.
   Anyway, the producers want to continue to make the movie that he had started to work on, but his page of notes with the plan of the movie on was covered in blood!
3. Show the students one of the activity sheets. Tell them it's their job to imagine what was under the blood stains and to plan the horror movie. They should write their new version on the clean part of the page.
4. Put students into pairs or small groups and give them an activity sheet. You may want to pair a weaker student with a stronger student for this task, or you may want to push the stronger students by pairing two strong students together.
5. Students work together to plan the horror movie. They will need careful monitoring and support during this stage. They should get as far as writing the dialogue for the opening scene.
6. When all the groups have finished, they should each tell the whole class about their movie. The class could vote on the best one.

Follow-up

- Students make the poster for the films they've created.
- Students role play the opening scene of the film, and if possible film it so you can watch it back. If you have time and equipment, they could dress up, use sound effects, write the opening titles on cards, etc.
- As students role play the first scene, ask them to change the genre. They can add to the dialogue but the basis should stay the same. They should change their actions and intonation as they perform the dialogue in the new genre.

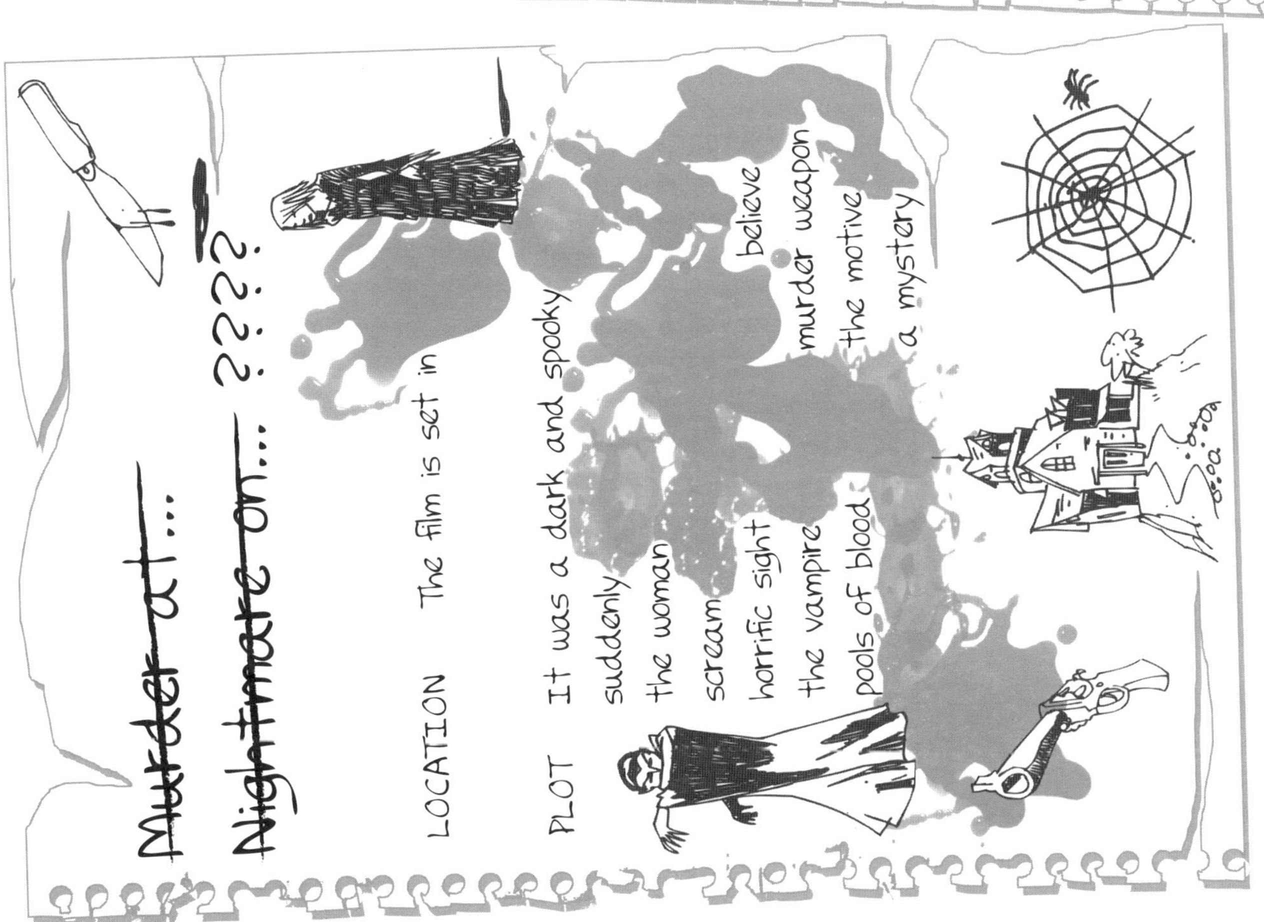

~~Murder at...~~
~~Nightmare on...~~ ????
LOCATION The film is set in
PLOT It was a dark and spooky
suddenly
the woman
scream
horrific sight
the vampire
pools of blood
believe
murder weapon
the motive
a mystery

LOCATION

MAIN CHARACTERS AND CAST

PLOT

THE OPENING SCENE

Takes place in

The atmosphere...

The characters...

THE OPENING DIALOGUE

Reality TV show

Language focus
informal, colloquial expressions

Key vocabulary
student-generated language from the role-play cards and colloquial phrases (see 'Catchphrases' on the role cards)

Skills focus
speaking: fluency – interacting in social situations

Level
upper-intermediate

Time
40 minutes

Preparation
one photocopy, cut up, for each group of 6 students

Warm-up

- Ask your students some of the following questions or write the questions on the board and ask students to find out the information about their partners.
  How many reality shows can you name?
  Which reality shows do you like / don't you like?
  Are reality shows popular in your country? Why / Why not?
  Would you ever consider taking part in a reality show? Why / Why not?

Main activity

1. Tell your students that they are going to take part in a *Big Brother* style reality show. *Big Brother* has been produced in over seventy countries so it is very likely your students will know all about it. Alternatively, if there is a reality show that is currently popular with your students, you could set the role-play in the setting of this popular show.
2. Explain to your students that at this stage in the show there are only six (or fewer if you don't have a number of students divisible by six) participants left in the house. Tell students they are going to play the roles of the six housemates.
3. With your students, think of a typical scene in the *Big Brother* house. The housemates could be making a meal or taking part in a challenge of some sort. Let your students think up the challenge. It could be as ridiculous as they like!
4. When all the participants understand the scenario, divide them into groups of six and give each group a set of role cards, one for each student. They should each read their role card and take a few minutes to think about how they are going to act. Each role card has two 'catchphrases' at the bottom. These are phrases that the contestant uses a lot in conversation. Tell the students they should try to incorporate the catchphrases into their role-play. For very high-level students, *insist* these phrases are used as it will add to the challenge.
5. If you have a camera, this would be a fun activity to film and watch back to simulate the real programme. Assign a cameraman or camerawoman. When you all watch the scene back, students should be given the task of listening for both good language and mistakes.
6. If you have students who would prefer to opt out of playing the roles, they could act as 'fly on the wall' error correctors and listen carefully to the role-play as it proceeds. Their job would be to make a note of any mistakes they hear. They could also make a note of any really good language they hear too. Then use their feedback afterwards in an error correction activity.

Follow-up

- Do a similar *Big Brother* role-play, but this time make it *Celebrity Big Brother.* Ask your students to write the character descriptions of some of their favourite celebrities. You could add the challenge that students have to guess who the famous people are by the way they behave and the clues they give as they talk to the other housemates.
- Write the following statements on the board for students to discuss.
  Reality shows are a waste of time and just a form of cheap television.
  Participants in reality shows are always attention-seekers.
  Watching reality shows is a good way to relax.
  I would love to take part in a reality show.
  Reality shows are addictive.

14.3 Reality TV show

You are a total fitness fanatic. You always have to be doing some sort of exercise. You are a vegetarian and only eat extremely healthy food. You want to win Big Brother so you can use the prize money to set up your own health and fitness centre. You are rather obsessed with telling other people that they should be exercising and eating healthily too!

Do you know how many calories are in that?
It's not good for you, you know!

You are the laziest person in the house! You love relaxing on the sofa and chatting to the other housemates. You try to do the minimum amount of housework, cooking, etc. You need at least ten hours sleep per night and you have been sleeping badly because your housemates talk all night. Right now, you are tired and grumpy!

Could you do me a little favour?
I'm shattered.

You are so nice! You are kind, helpful, always ready to do the cooking or the housework. You are a good listener and you think you get on really well with everybody in the house. In fact, you think you are now so popular that you are starting to worry that your housemates may vote for you to leave the house so they have more chance of winning.

Do you want a shoulder to cry on?
Do you need a hand?

You have very strong opinions about everything and you are not afraid of speaking your mind. You find it hard to listen to other people's ideas and you like to be the centre of attention. You like order and you naturally try to organise all the housemates so that the house is well organised and tidy.

Well, I'll tell you what I think …
This house is a mess!

You are a very laid-back person. You don't mind if the house is untidy or the meals are late. You believe in the saying 'Live and let live' and you try not to bother your housemates. You are a vegetarian and don't like to hear your housemates arguing.

Why don't we just chill out?
Peace, man!

You are a sociologist and you are taking part in Big Brother so you can write about the phenomenon of reality shows for your thesis as part of your degree. Your housemates don't know this, but you are observing their every move and action. You try to provoke difficult situations so that you have lots to write about in your thesis on human nature.

You're not going to believe what I just saw!
I shouldn't really tell you this, but …

Fortune teller

Language focus
will/won't for predicting the future

Key vocabulary
star signs, numbers, colours, months and the alphabet

Skills focus
speaking: asking questions, making predictions and spelling

Level
elementary

Time
45 minutes

Preparation
one photocopy for each student; either cut them to the correct size, or provide students with scissors

Warm-up

- Collect some pictures that represent the twelve star signs. These are easily found on the Internet. Show them to your students one by one, asking which sign they represent. Check your students' pronunciation of the signs and elicit the dates for the signs. This will provide good practice in ordinal numbers and months. Stick them on the board and write the corresponding dates next to them.

  The star signs in English are: *Aries* /eəriːz/ March 21st – April 20th, *Taurus* /tɔːrəs/ April 21st – May 21st, *Gemini* /ˈdʒemɪnaɪ/ May 22nd – June 22nd, *Cancer* /kænsə/ June 23rd – July 23rd, *Leo* /liːəʊ/ July 24th – August 23rd, *Virgo* /ˈvɜːgəʊ/ August 24th – September 23rd, *Libra* /liːbrə/ September 24th – October 23rd, *Scorpio* /skɔːpiəʊ/ October 24th – November 22nd, *Sagittarius* /sædʒɪteəriəs/ November 23rd – December 22nd, *Capricorn* /kæprɪkɔːn/ December 23rd – January 19th, *Aquarius* /əˈkweəriəs/ January 20th – February 19th and *Pisces* /paɪsiːz/ February 20th – March 20th.

Main activity

1. Ask students if they would like to know more about their futures. What questions would they ask a fortune teller? Write the questions on the board. For example: *Will I be famous? Will I have a good job? Will I live to be 100? Will I pass the English exam next week? Will I meet Brad Pitt one day?*
2. Give each student an activity sheet and follow the instructions to make the fortune tellers together as a class. Demonstrate each stage to students before they do it. Then demonstrate how it works with a student. Check students understand all the language on the fortune teller.
3. When everyone has a fortune teller, put students into pairs. They should take it in turns to tell each other's fortunes. First, the fortune teller asks the 'client' one of the questions in the four circles. When they choose a colour, month, number or star sign these need to be spelt out by the fortune teller. Each letter corresponds to one open/close of the fortune teller. For example, 'S-C-O-R-P-I-O' – the student reads out the letters as he/she opens and closes the fortune teller.
4. Then the client has to make a question with *will*. The fortune teller can decide on the answer, by saying, '*I think you will!* or *I don't think you will!* As they give their answer, each word corresponds to an opening and closing of the fortune teller, to reveal the next set of questions.
5. Now the client should make another question with *will*. This time the fortune teller opens the flap to reveal the answer.
6. When students have had turns at being both the fortune teller and the client, ask some of the students what the future holds for them, or ask them all to write a summary of the predictions and say whether or not they believe them!

Follow-up

- Write a page of horoscopes with your class. Give each pair or group a star sign to write predictions for. Put them all together to display on the notice board.
- Look in magazines, newspapers or on the Internet for examples of horoscopes in English. Students read the predictions for their star sign (with the help of a dictionary or your support) and decide if they would like to believe them or not.

15.1 Fortune teller

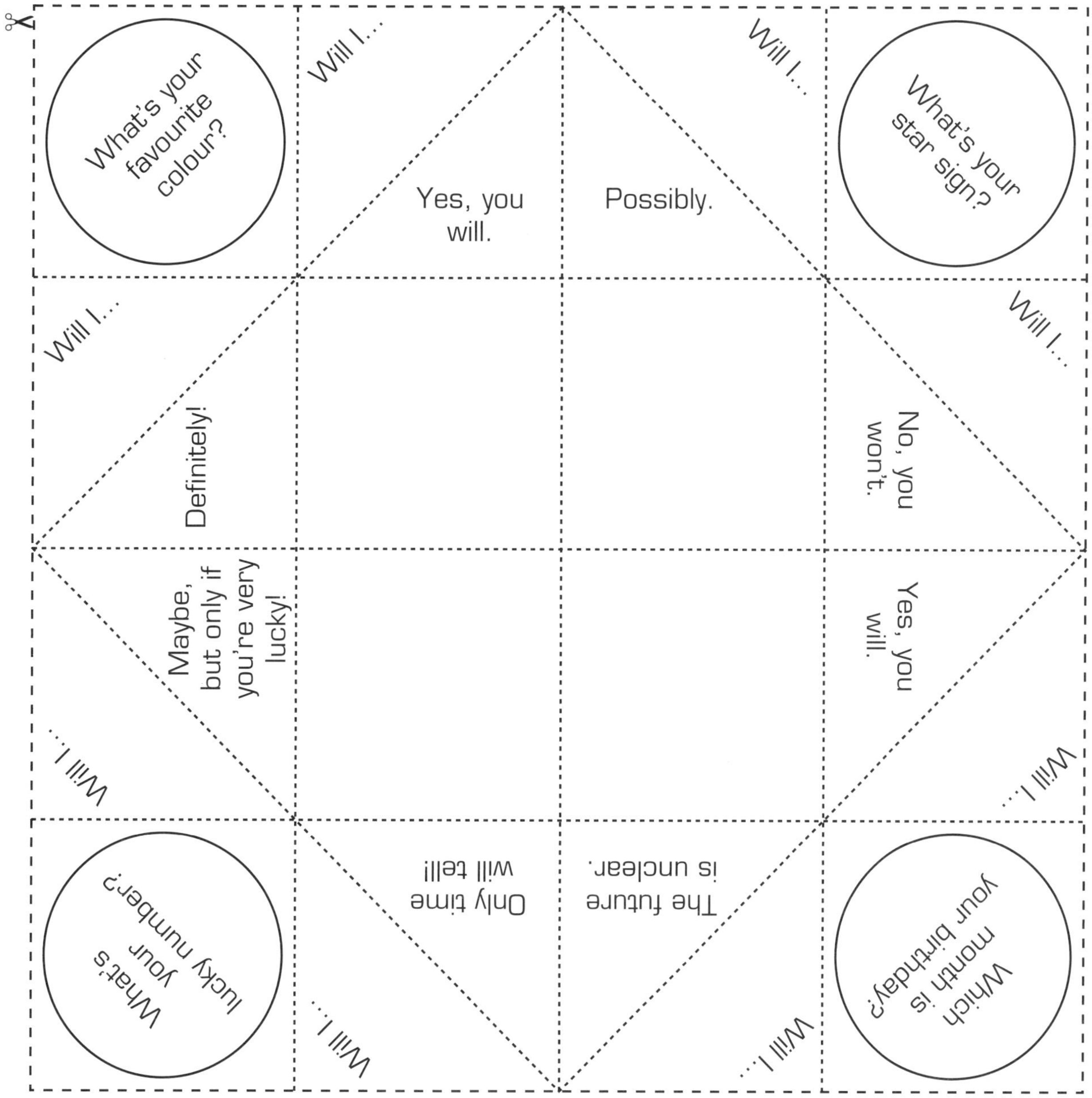

What's your favourite colour?

Will I …

Yes, you will.

Possibly.

Will I …

What's your star sign?

Will I …

Definitely!

Will I …

No, you won't.

Maybe, but only if you're very lucky!

Yes, you will.

Will I …

Will I …

What's your lucky number?

Only time will tell!

The future is unclear.

Which month is your birthday?

Will I …

Will I …

How to make your fortune teller

1. Complete the eight 'Will …' questions.
2. Put the fortune teller on the table, face down.
3. Fold it in half, then in half again, then unfold.
4. Still face down, fold the corners into the middle to make a smaller square.
5. Turn it over and fold all the corners into the middle again to make an even smaller square.
6. Fold in half, and half again, then unfold.
7. Put your index fingers and thumbs under the paper flaps.
8. Move your fingers north to south, then east to west to open and close the fortune teller.

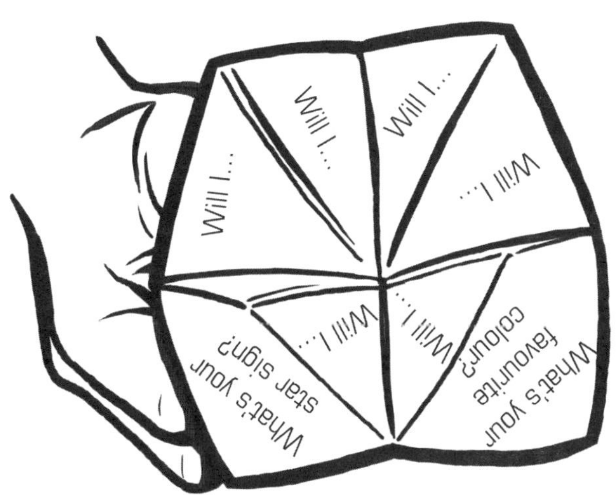

Will I…
Will I…
Will I…
Will I…
Will I…
Will I…
What's your star sign?
What's your favourite colour?

Vote for me

Language focus
first conditional

Key vocabulary
political policies

Skills focus
writing: targeting an audience
speaking: persuading and convincing others

Level
intermediate

Time
50 minutes

Preparation
one photocopy, cut up, for every group of 3 or 4 students; a small piece of blank 'voting' paper for each student; a bag or box to put the voting papers in

Extra notes
This activity would be ideal to do when there are local or general elections being held where you are teaching.

Warm-up

1. Ask students how old they have to be in their country to do certain things like learn to drive, buy cigarettes or alcohol, leave school, and vote. When they tell you the age limits, ask your students if they think the age limits are right. Do they think they're fair? Why / Why not?
2. Focus on the voting age and ask students if they would like to change it.

Main activity

1. Ask students to imagine that the age limit for voting has been changed to thirteen. Ask them what policies they think would make teenagers vote for a certain politician. You could write their ideas on the board.
2. Put students into groups of three or four and give each group a copy of the top half of the activity sheet – Sara Bear's election poster. Ask them to read it quickly and then ask if any of the policies they had previously predicted are there.
3. Ask them which policies on the poster they think are the most important and to choose the top three. When groups have done this, ask them to compare their answers with another group or ask the class for some feedback.
4. Now give each group the blank election poster on the bottom half of the activity sheet. Tell them that they are going to work in their groups to think up a name for a new political party for young people. They should also think of a name for the politician and put a photo of him or her (this could be a picture from a magazine) or draw a picture in the space. The group should also write down the policies the party has and add a slogan in the banner at the bottom of the page.
5. When all the groups have finished, each group should present their ideas to the whole class as if they have all got a three-minute slot on television to advertise their party and their policies. One member of the group can take the role of the politician and the others can be in their team of supporters. Write up the following phrases on the board to help the 'politicians' really try and sell themselves to the other groups.
   If you vote for us, we will ...
   If you choose us, we will ...
   If we win this election, we will ...
   We are the best choice because ...
   Be a winner and vote for us!
   Make the right choice, vote for us!
   (See Follow-up for optional step.)
6. When each group has presented their party, hold a class vote to decide on which party would be the best option for teenagers to vote for. Hold a secret ballot by giving students a piece of blank paper each. They should write the name of their favourite party on the paper and put it in a box, bag or envelope. Then ask some of your students to count up the votes and present the results.

Follow-up

- After each 'party' has presented their policies (Main activity: Step 5), before students vote, hold a press conference, where each 'party' in turn should sit facing the class and the others have to think of questions they'd like to ask them to justify their policies and their plans for the future.
- Students make a TV or radio news report to give the results of the class election. They could produce graphic illustrations such as bar charts or pie charts to show the results and then explain them.

If we win the elections …

- ★ … we will give a free laptop computer to all students aged 13 and above.
- ★ … we will reduce the car driving age to 15 and small motorbikes to 13.
- ★ … we will build more youth centres with skate parks.
- ★ … we will give you points for attending school. Students can exchange points for prizes – summer courses, books, sports equipment, etc.
- ★ … we will reduce the legal age for having tattoos to 13. We believe you are old enough to decide.

Sara
Bear
HFY

★ ***So, make the right choice and vote for the HOPE FOR YOUTH party.***

If we win the elections …

- ★ … we will
- ★ …
- ★ …
- ★ …
- ★ …
- ★ …

★

The walk of life

Language focus
tense revision

Key vocabulary
to age, to become older, to get old, newborn, to speed up time, toddler, to turn back time

Skills focus
speaking: expressing opinions – speaking for one minute

Level
upper-intermediate

Time
40 minutes

Preparation
one photocopy for each group of 4 students; a dice per group; a counter for each student (e.g. a paper clip, rubber or pencil sharpener)

Extra notes
If your students are preparing for any formal examinations in English, this task may be good practice for any individual speaking turn they may have in the oral exam.

Warm-up

1. Revise language of growing up by asking students what you would call people of the following ages:

0–4 months	newborn baby
4–18 months	baby
18 months–2 years	toddler
2 years–12 years	child
13–19 years	teenager
20–29 years	adult – in his/her twenties
30–39 years	adult – in his/her thirties
40–49 years	adult – in his/her forties
50–59 years	adult – in his/her fifties
60–65 years	adult – in his/her sixties
65+	retired, pensioner
70+	old/elderly person, pensioner

2. You could have a race to the board in teams, where you say an age and students race to write the correct word on the board. The age limits aren't set in stone for the babies, so be flexible with the students' answers.

Main activity

1. Give one board game to each group of four students. They will need a dice and a counter each. For counters they can use any small item from their pencil cases.
2. When it is their turn, they throw the dice to decide how many spaces they move. They must then talk for a minute to answer the question they land on. If they don't succeed, they must go back to where they came from.
3. As students play the game, the other team members are in charge of timing the minute and deciding if the player did well enough to stay where they are on the board. If there are too many hesitations and pauses for thinking time, the student should move back.
4. The winner is the first student to reach the finish.
5. This activity gives students the chance to practise a lot of different tenses. It may be a good idea to monitor the students as they're speaking and later on do some error correction of the most common mistakes.

Follow-up

- Cut pictures out of magazines and make a wall chart of the ageing process. The pictures should illustrate newborn through to a very old person. Under each picture the students write about the advantages and disadvantages of each age.
- Hold a class debate using some of the topics that have been touched upon during the game. Use the four discussion statements from the game board (squares 3, 8, 16 and 20) to hold a class debate.

15.3 The walk of life

START
1 Who's the youngest person you know? Describe him or her.
2 What's your first memory as a child?
3 Do you think that we'll be able to live forever one day?
4 Do you think that time passes faster, as you get older?
5 If you could turn back time and become younger, would you? Why?
6 What's the best age to be? Why?
7 What do you think you'll be doing in ten years' time?
8 'In the future we'll be able to live forever.' Discuss
9 What has the happiest time of your life been so far?
10 Do old people in your country generally have a good life?
11 If you could take a pill and stay the age you are now, forever, would you? Why? Why not?
12 Who's the oldest person you know? Describe him or her.
13 Where do you think you'll be living in fifty years' time?
14 'The teenage years are the best.' Discuss.
15 How do you imagine your life when you're thirty years old?
16 'Youth is wasted on the young.' Discuss.
17 In the future, would you have plastic surgery? Why?
18 'You're only as old as you feel.' Discuss.
19 If you could speed up time and become older faster, would you? Why?
20 How do you imagine your life to be in twenty years' time?
21 RELAX! You're getting old!
RELAX
22 Do you think you're always going to feel the same on the inside, as you get older?
FINISH
R.I.P
E.Hedgwig
1895 - 1997

Get the message across

Language focus
introduction to basic functional travel language

Key vocabulary
travel: *airport, bag, baggage, bus, delay, hotel, lost, money, police station, restaurant, shop, street, towel, train station*

Skills focus
speaking: getting your meaning across; writing a dialogue

Level
elementary

Time
60 minutes

Preparation
one photocopy, cut up, for every group of 5 or 6 students; blank scrap paper for each student to use for drawing

Extra notes
This activity can be used with higher levels too to revise functional travel language.

Warm-up

1. Divide the board into two areas, A and B, and put students into two teams.
2. Invite one member of team A to come to the board, and give them a list of words to draw. (They are not allowed to speak, but they may also mime.) Words should be connected to the topic of travel and could include the following: *aeroplane, boat, car, train, bus, taxi, suitcase, bag, rucksack, airport, train station, hotel, restaurant, map, beach, mountains, sunglasses, hat, towel.*
3. Set a time limit of two minutes. The team members should guess the words being drawn and get a point for each word they guess within the time.
4. Then it is team B's turn to do the same.

Main activity

1. Put students into teams of five or six and give each team a set of cards. Tell them that each card depicts a problem they may have when travelling abroad.
2. Students take it in turns to pick a card, look at the picture and communicate the message in the picture to their team. The team have to guess where they are and what the problem is. For the first round the students can only use mime and drawing. They mustn't speak! The team must guess the situation and the problem in English only.

Answers

1 The airline has lost her bag.
2 He wants to know where he can find the bus stops.
3 She wants to know where the Museum of Modern Art is.
4 She is asking where she can find a cash machine.
5 She is asking for a wake-up call.
6 He has no cash and wants to know if he can pay by credit card.
7 He wants to know what time the train to Birmingham will leave.
8 He is reporting the theft of his rucksack, containing his wallet and passport.

3. When all the cards have been used up and the teams have guessed the situations and the problems for each card, put students into pairs and give each pair one card.
4. Now students are going to focus on one situation in pairs and write a short and simple dialogue for the situation. They can also use mime and drawing to support the language they have. Tell students that you *don't* expect them to have all the language they need to do this but encourage them to ask you for useful language chunks and vocabulary. Your role at this stage will be to feed in new language and to encourage students to be creative with the language and other resources they have. If your students are very low level, explain that vocabulary is much more important in order to communicate than grammar. Also point out that actions can be substituted for many words, so encourage students to use body language.
5. When the pairs have produced and practised their dialogues they could perform them for the class.

Follow-up

- Ask your students to think about more situations when they may need to use English. Each student should draw (or write in L1) a situation. Use the cards for another team game in a following class.
- When your students have had more practice with functional travel language, use the picture cards as prompts for role play in a later class.

16.1

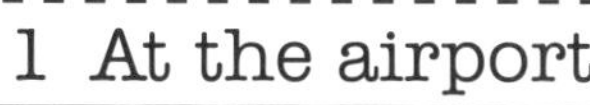
Get the message across

1 At the airport

2 At the airport

3 In the street

MUSEAM OF
MODERN ART
MAP

4 In the street

CASH

5 At the hotel

7:00am

6 In a restaurant

7 At the train station

information
DEPARTURES
TIME
LONDON
12:00
BIRMINGHAM
DELAYED
GLASGOW
12:30

8 At the police station

Café
PASSPORT

English abroad

Language focus
agreeing and disagreeing: *I agree with you because … ; I totally disagree with you … ; Don't you think …?*
expressing preferences: *would; I'd prefer to go to … because …*
travel

Key vocabulary
accommodation, to book, booking form, camp site, excursions, to get bored, home stay, reservation form, weekend trips

Skills focus
reading: extracting key information
speaking: discussing pros and cons

Level
intermediate

Time
45 minutes

Preparation
one photocopy for each pair of students; a map of the world for the warm-up

Warm-up

1. Show students a map of the world and ask them which countries in the world speak English as a first language (UK, USA, Canada, New Zealand, Australia and Ireland) and which countries have English as an official language (India, Sri Lanka, Pakistan and South Africa). (Many other countries – approximately seventy-five – have English as an official language or a language with a special status; these are simply the main ones.)
2. Ask volunteer students to come up and point to these countries on the map. This will naturally lead on to students telling you about any experiences they may have had in the English-speaking countries mentioned.

Main activity

1. If any of your students have ever been on summer courses abroad to learn English, use their personal experiences to enrich this class. Ask the rest of the class to ask them some questions about their experiences in small groups and to find out as much as possible about their time abroad.
2. If you feel it is necessary, revise language of agreeing and disagreeing and expressing preferences before you begin.
3. Tell students that you want them to imagine they are going to do a summer course for one month in an English-speaking country. Where would they like to go? Listen to students' initial opinions.
4. Then put students into pairs and ask them to read the adverts for the four language courses. To extend the challenge, give each student two adverts to read and then tell their partner about.
5. Now, students should discuss the pros and cons of studying English in each of the four countries. They can use their prior knowledge as well as the information given in the adverts. For example: *I wouldn't like to go to England because my cousin went there last year and she said the food was terrible!*
6. If you have access to the Internet, your students could do some further research into the countries before making their decisions. If they type the name of the country and 'tourist information' into a search engine they should find plenty of relevant pages with photos and simple descriptions of the highlights of each place.
7. When they have decided where they would like to go, you could extend the task by saying that the whole class have to go to the same country. Students now need to persuade each other to choose their own preferred destination.

Follow-up

- Ask students to imagine that they have been on the summer course to one of the countries and they have just arrived home. Students prepare the conversation with a friend who is asking all about their trip. They will need time to think up questions to ask each other and to invent things they did during the trip. You could divide the class in two and tell half the class they had a wonderful trip and the other half they had a terrible trip.
- Students imagine they are in the English-speaking country. They write a postcard back to an English-speaking friend or to you, their English teacher, explaining how the course is going.

16.2 English abroad

Study English in NEW ZEALAND with our special English Adventure courses.

If you like outdoor adventure activities and fresh air, New Zealand is for you. Learn English in the mornings, and in the afternoons choose from mountain walking, rafting, bungee jumping, skiing, whale-watching or diving.

Accommodation: Campsite or backpacker hostels

For more information e-mail jon@nz4adventure.com

Where better to learn English than in the UK?

Choose from our schools in all the capital cities of the UK – London, Edinburgh, Cardiff or Belfast – or our schools in the country. You won't get bored on our courses! We offer weekend trips to other cities, excursions to castles, museums, concerts, etc.

UNDERGROUND

Accommodation: Homestay (all meals included)

To book, fill in our on-line reservation form at: www.uk4english.co.uk

Stand out from the crowd – take an English course in SOUTH AFRICA

Come to Cape Town to learn English for an experience of a lifetime. Cape Town is a cosmopolitan and vibrant city, buzzing with life. When you're not studying, take trips to explore the African wildlife on safari, or learn to dive or surf.

Accommodation: 3, 4 or 5 star hotels

For more information e-mail: Jackie@capetownschool.sa

Experience living in the USA by studying English with us this summer

We have special courses for teenagers in New York, Boston and Chicago. Meet teenagers from all over the world and study the 'real' English you hear in the movies! Afternoon activities include sports, excursions and visiting local places of interest.

Accommodation: Individual or shared bedroom on college campus

For more information and the booking form go to our website: www.stateseng.net

Gap year blog

Language focus
mixed conditionals

Key vocabulary
apprentice, to be shattered, charity, to post photos (to a blog), round-the-world ticket, to take a gap year, to volunteer, working holiday

Skills focus
reading: understanding main ideas
speaking: discussing options
writing: a blog

Level
upper-intermediate

Time
60 minutes

Preparation
one photocopy, cut up, for each student

Extra notes
In the UK it is very common for students to take a 'gap year' before starting university. Many universities prefer to take students who have taken a gap year as they believe it gives students the opportunity to become more independent and to learn new skills.

Warm-up

- Ask students to think of advantages and disadvantages of a gap year – a 'year out' – between school and university. Advantages: *It's a chance to see the world, an opportunity to learn or practise a foreign language, it gives you time to decide what you want to do at university, a chance to be independent.* Disadvantages: *It can be expensive, you may miss your friends and family, it may be difficult to organise.*

Main activity

1. Ask students to imagine the scenario of a student who takes a gap year and travels to the other side of the world to work. Ask the class how he/she will keep in touch with family and friends at home. If nobody suggests writing a travel blog, then tell students a little about blogs and if possible show some examples of travel blogs from the Internet. Type 'Travel Blogs' into a search engine and you will find plenty of examples.
2. Put students into pairs and give each student a copy of Clare's gap year travel blog to read.
3. Now ask the pairs of students to think of two questions they'd like to ask Clare and write them in the 'Message board and questions' space on the blog.
4. As the pairs finish, put two pairs together to make a group of four and ask them to swap their travel blog with the other pair. Ask them to imagine they are Clare and to write an answer next to the questions they've been asked.
5. When both pairs have finished, they should return the blogs to the original pair to read the replies. At this stage, ask the whole class for some feedback about the questions and answers.
6. Now, leave students in their new groups of four. Give each group a set of gap year option cards. Ask them to decide which option they would prefer to do. They can add in any details or say how they would adapt the options to suit their preferences.
7. When they have decided, ask some of them to explain and justify their choices.
8. Then ask students to imagine that they really are doing the gap year activity they chose and to imagine that they are writing about their experiences on a travel blog. Students now write a posting to their blog.
9. When all the students have written a blog posting, pass them around so the students can read one another's blogs and write questions to the authors.

Follow-up

Use the idea of gap years to role play any of the following scenarios.

- You want to take a gap year. Try to convince your parents that it's a good idea! (To do in pairs or groups of three with one student and one or two parents)
- You have just come home from taking a gap year where you lived in a country with a very different culture from your own. Talk to your parents about the things you really missed. (Student and one or two parents)
- Give each group a map of the world. Ask them to plan their ideal world trip. If you like, limit the destinations to ten. Each group explains their itinerary to the whole class.

16.3 Gap year blog

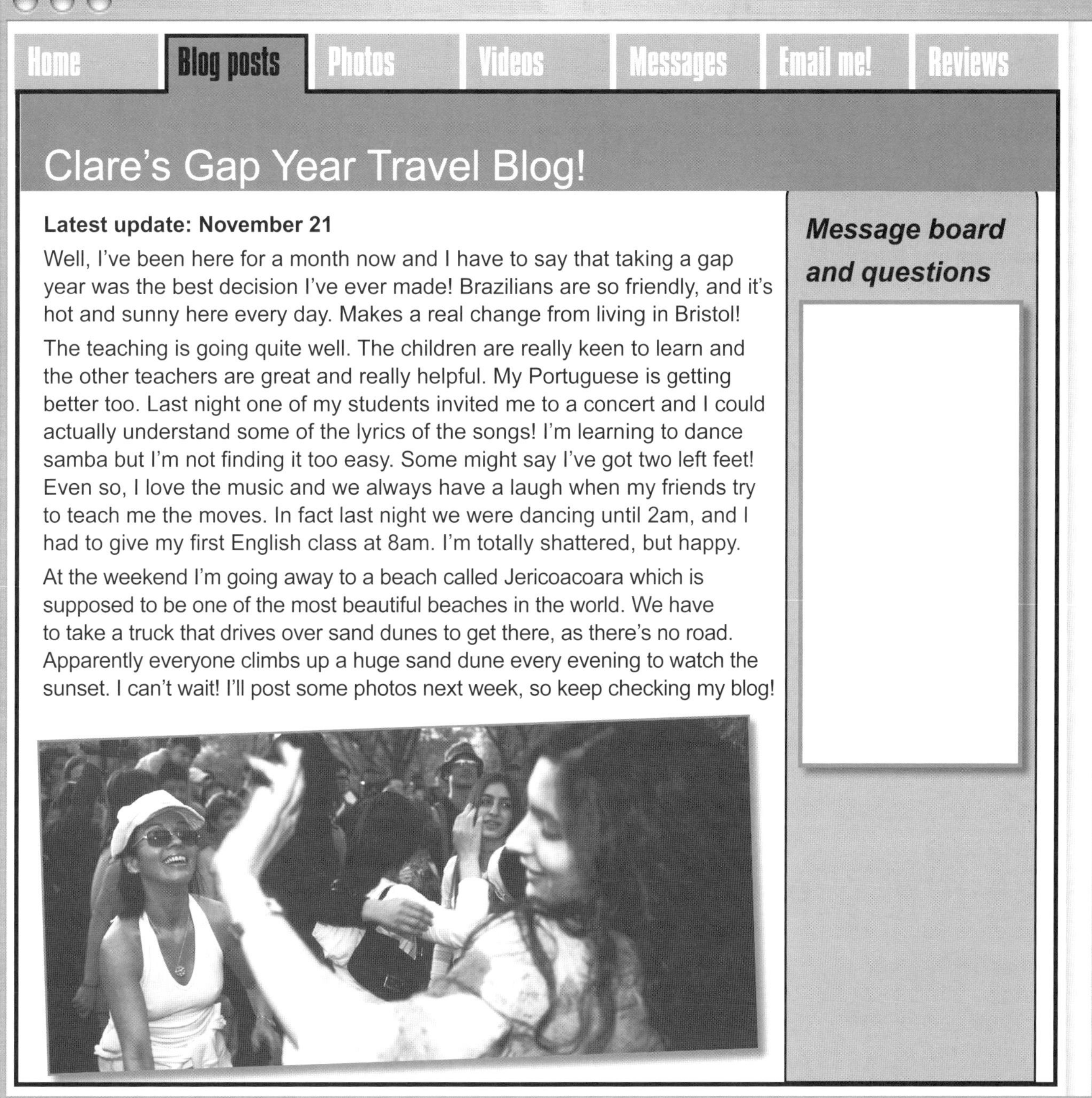

Home
Blog posts
Photos
Videos
Messages
Email me!
Reviews
Clare's Gap Year Travel Blog!
Latest update: November 21
Well, I've been here for a month now and I have to say that taking a gap year was the best decision I've ever made! Brazilians are so friendly, and it's hot and sunny here every day. Makes a real change from living in Bristol!
The teaching is going quite well. The children are really keen to learn and the other teachers are great and really helpful. My Portuguese is getting better too. Last night one of my students invited me to a concert and I could actually understand some of the lyrics of the songs! I'm learning to dance samba but I'm not finding it too easy. Some might say I've got two left feet! Even so, I love the music and we always have a laugh when my friends try to teach me the moves. In fact last night we were dancing until 2am, and I had to give my first English class at 8am. I'm totally shattered, but happy.
At the weekend I'm going away to a beach called Jericoacoara which is supposed to be one of the most beautiful beaches in the world. We have to take a truck that drives over sand dunes to get there, as there's no road. Apparently everyone climbs up a huge sand dune every evening to watch the sunset. I can't wait! I'll post some photos next week, so keep checking my blog!
Message board and questions

Option 1	Option 2	Option 3	Option 4
Work for six months in your own country to earn some money, then buy a round-the-world ticket! Choose your favourite destinations and experience the pure joy of travelling!	Volunteer for an organisation that works with children. Help out in schools and hospitals, teaching your language, entertaining children or building new schools.	Work your way around the world! Travel around Australia and really get to know it by working as you travel. You could do fruit picking, restaurant work, farm work, etc. When you have earned the money you need, keep travelling!	Use your gap year to get work experience in your own country. Either volunteer to work for a charity or work as an apprentice in the area that you are most interested in. Employers like people who have work experience.

Recycling race

Language focus
singular and plural forms: *It's a* / *They're …*; *It's* / *They're made of …*; *It goes* / *They go …*

Key vocabulary
recycling: *bottle, box, can, container, glass, jar, metal, packet, paper, plastic, plastic bag, to reuse, rubbish, tin*
games language: *counter, miss a turn, move on two squares, throw again*

Skills focus
speaking: giving information

Level
elementary

Time
50 minutes

Preparation
one photocopy, cut up, of the picture cards (page 107) and one (enlarged if possible) photocopy of the game board (page 108) and a coin for every group of 3 to 6 students; a counter for each student; for the Warm-up – a bag of clean recyclable rubbish (or pictures of items that could be recycled)

Extra notes
This game would complement any coursebook topic or project work about the environment.

Warm-up

1. Bring in a bag of clean recyclable rubbish. (Alternatively, use pictures.) Ask students to guess what's in your rubbish bag and to ask questions about it before you start taking items out. Ensure you have more than one of several items. As you pull out each item ask students *What's this?* to elicit the structure *It's a …* and *What are these?* to elicit the structure *They're …* .
2. Use the items in your rubbish bag, or ones that you have drawn on the board, to check that students know the vocabulary they will need to play the game – *bottle, can, tin, box, jar, plastic, paper, metal* and *glass*.

Main activity

1. Show students cards (page 107) and the game board (page 108) . Draw their attention to the recycling containers on the game board and explain that the 'special items' container is for things that are made of mixed materials that need special attention to recycle. Ask students to think of an item for each container. Hold up several picture cards and ask students *What's this? / What are these? What's it / What are they made of?* and *Where does it / do they go?* For example *It's a bottle, it's made of plastic and it goes in the packaging container.* Repeat the questions until you are satisfied that students are confident with the structures and understand what types of thing can go in each of the recycling containers.
2. Divide the class into teams of between three and six and give each team one set of cards and a board. They should put all the shuffled cards face down in the card space in the middle of the board. Each student will need a counter and each group a coin. The idea is to get around the board from start to finish. Students use the coin instead of a dice (heads = 2, tails =1).
3. To play, students take it in turns to toss the coin, move along the board and take a card. If the card is a picture card, they have to say what it is and which container it goes in. If the other students in the group all agree that the sentence is correct, the student stays where they are on the board, but if they get it wrong they go back to where they were. If they get a message card, they should do what it tells them.
4. The winner is the first person to reach the finish square.

Answers
Paper container: a newspaper, cardboard boxes, a magazine, magazines
Packaging, plastic and metal container: a tin, tins, a can, cans, bottles
Glass container: a bottle, a jar, jars
Special items container: a light bulb, a computer, CDs, batteries

Follow-up

- Students make a poster to encourage their classmates to recycle more. Ask students to collect packaging to make a collage for part of the poster. They should think of a slogan for their recycling campaign. If possible, display the posters in the corridor or in the classroom.
- Students do a class survey to find out who recycles the most in the class.
- Ask students to think of other things they can do to help the environment, apart from recycling their waste. Rank them in order from the most to the least important, according to your students.

17.1 Recycling race

TOMATOS

AA
AA

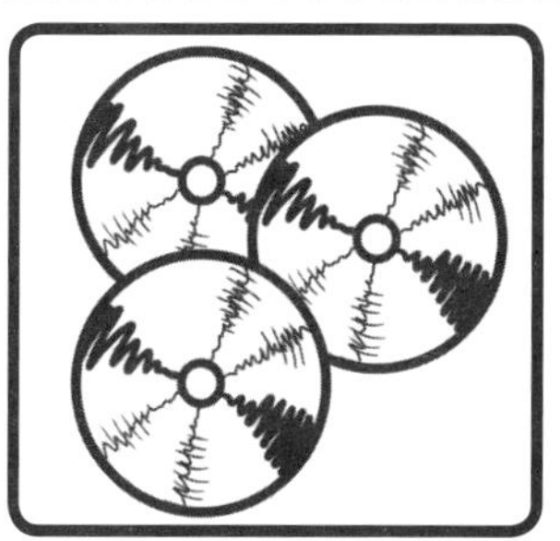

DAILY NEWS
GREAT NEWS

JAM

TOMATOS

MAGAZINE

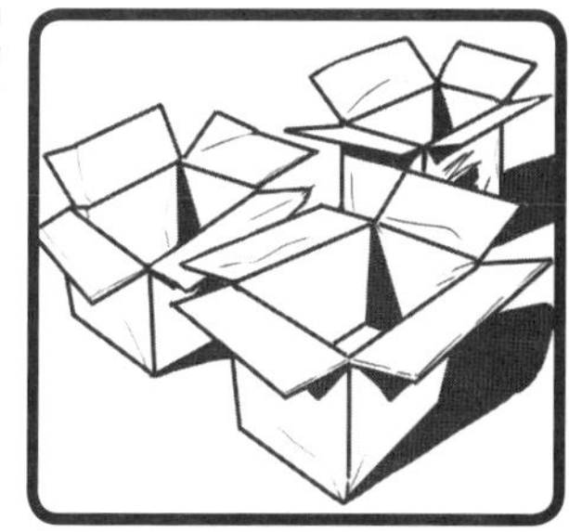

SPA

OLIVES

You feel lazy and put all your rubbish in the bin. Miss a turn.	You ask your school to recycle their paper. Move on two squares.	You always reuse plastic bags. Move on two squares.	You say 'No' to plastic bags when you're shopping. Move on two squares.
You always try to recyclc your rubbish. Move on two squares.	You always use both sides of sheets of paper. Move on two squares.	It's too far to walk to the recycling containers so you put your rubbish in the bin. Miss a turn.	You always take plastic bags from shops and you don't reuse them. Miss a turn.

17.1 Recycling race

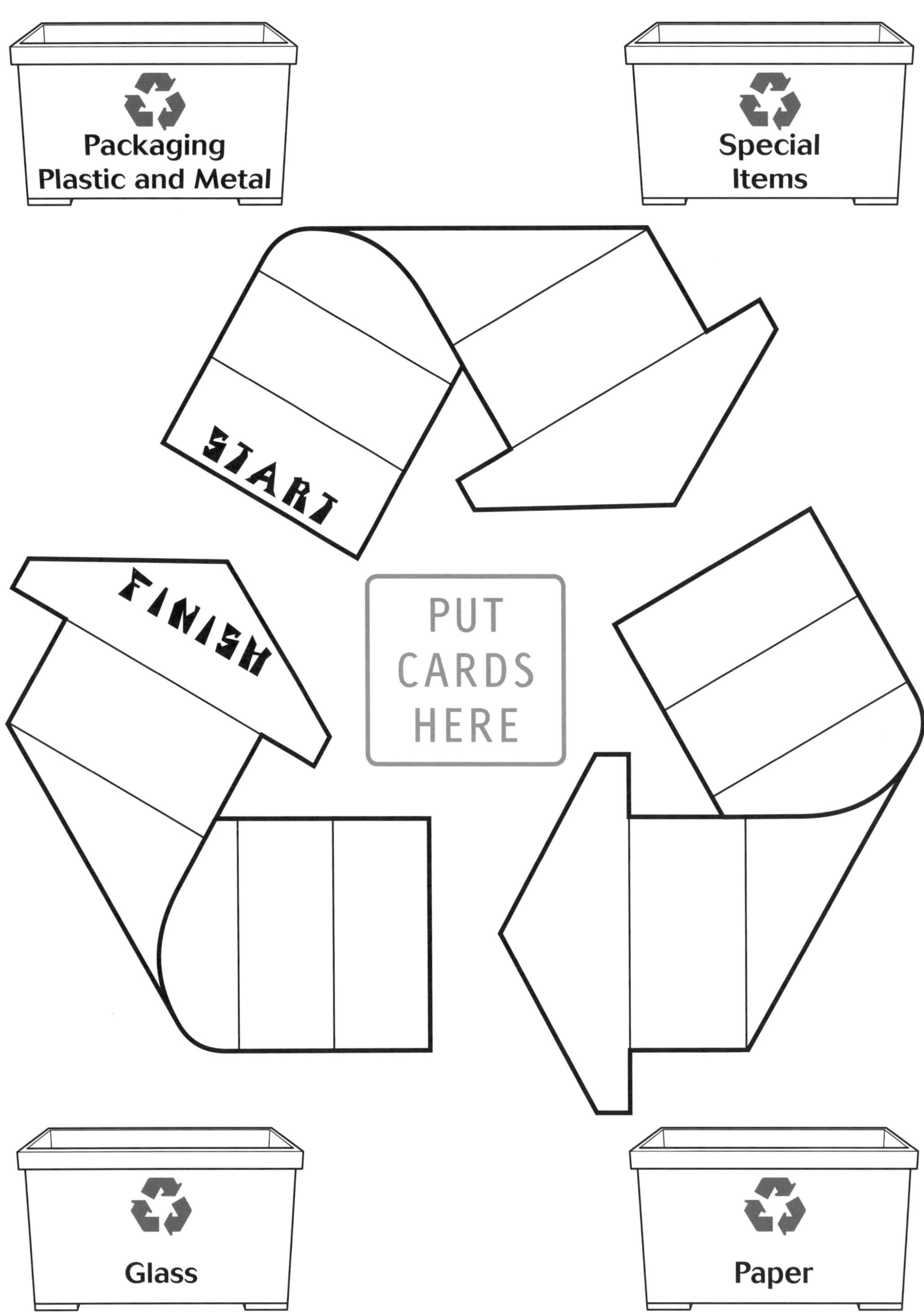

Packaging
Plastic and Metal
Special
Items
START
FINISH
PUT
CARDS
HERE
Glass
Paper

Ecological footprint

Language focus
adverbs of frequency

Key vocabulary
the environment: *electrical appliance, fast food, lifestyle, plastic bag, processed food, to recycle, to turn off, vegetarian*

Skills focus
reading: answering questions
speaking: comparing

Level
intermediate

Time
60 minutes

Preparation
one photocopy for each group of 3 or 4 students

Warm-up

1. Play a 'guess what I'm drawing' game. Divide the class into two teams, and each team takes turns to nominate an artist. Give the artist an item to draw on the board and both teams must try to guess the word.
2. The first team to guess correctly wins a point. Words to include for this game are: *aeroplane, car, pollution, traffic jam, packaging, fast food, recycling, electricity, electrical appliances, vegetarian, turn on* or *turn off.*

Main activity

1. Divide the class into groups of three or four and give each group an activity sheet. Ask students to look at the pictures at the top of the page and to read about Ben and Jessica and answer the questions below.

   Answers
   1 Jessica's. She uses less energy and resources.
   2 Ben's.

2. Ask students whether or not they have heard about 'ecological footprints' before and if so, what do they know about them? Ask them to read the boxed definition of an ecological footprint on their activity sheet. If the concept is new to them, ensure that they understand that the bigger the footprint, the bigger the damage to the environment. The term was first coined in 1992 by Canadian ecologist, William Rees. If the concept of the ecological footprint is new to you, type 'ecological footprint' into a search engine on the Internet where you will find websites that explain the idea and offer calculators so you can work out your own ecological footprint.
3. Ask students what type of activities make big 'ecological footprints'. Elicit activities like leaving lights on, using lots of energy, driving cars, travelling by plane, wasting water, etc.
4. In their groups, students do the quiz. Each group should have one 'quizmaster' who reads out the questions to the group and one 'scorer' who makes a note of everybody's answers. These roles can change halfway through so everyone takes a role at some point through the task.
5. When they have finished, ask students to compare their results. Then get each group to feed back to the rest of the class.

Follow-up

- Ask students to think of other questions to include in the 'ecological footprint' quiz. Students write five more questions to ask each other.
- Students make a poster to encourage their peers to think about the environment in their everyday activities.
- If you want to follow on with the idea of the 'ecological footprint', students could draw around their feet and write an environmental tip inside the footprint. These could be assembled on the classroom wall in the shape of a tree or a flower.

17.2 Ecological footprint

Hi! I'm Ben. I come to school by motorbike and my mum always gets angry because I always forget to switch off the lights, the computer and the TV. My dad lives in Australia and I always go to see him in the school holidays. I love fast food and I eat meat every day.

Hi! I'm Jessica. I walk to school and I always try to remember to switch off the lights and the TV at home. When we go on holiday we usually go to see my grandparents who live in Wales. We always go by train. I'm a vegetarian and I love cooking.

1 Whose lifestyle is better for the environment? Why?
2 Whose lifestyle uses a lot of energy?

Our 'ecological footprint' is how much land we need to give us the energy and resources for our lifestyle. The more energy and resources you use, the bigger your 'ecological footprint'.

Ecological footprint quiz

How big is your ecological footprint? Do this quiz and find out.

1 How often do you eat meat or fish?
- A Once or twice a week.
- B Most days.
- C Hardly ever.

2 How often do you eat fast food or processed food?
- A Hardly ever.
- B Often.
- C Sometimes.

3 How often do you travel by car?
- A Most days.
- B Never.
- C Not often.

4 How many electrical appliances do you have in your bedroom?
- A One or two.
- B More than five.
- C Between two and five.

5 Do you always turn off the TV, computer and lights when you're not using them?
- A Yes, I always turn them off.
- B No, I always leave things on.
- C No, I sometimes leave them on.

6 How many hours do you spend flying in an aeroplane in an average year?
- A Less than ten.
- B I hardly ever fly.
- C More than ten.

7 How often do you travel by bike or on foot?
- A Sometimes.
- B Every day.
- C Hardly ever.

8 Do you recycle old paper, glass and plastic?
- A Always.
- B Sometimes.
- C Never.

9 When you go to the supermarket, how do you carry the shopping home?
- A In the plastic bag from the supermarket.
- B In my own bag, rucksack or basket I bring with me.
- C In an old plastic bag that I reuse.

10 Which do you have most often?
- A A deep bath.
- B A long shower.
- C A quick shower.

Calculate your score

1	A = 2	B = 3	C = 1	6	A = 2	B = 1	C = 3
2	A = 1	B = 3	C = 2	7	A = 2	B = 0	C = 3
3	A = 3	B = 0	C = 2	8	A = 0	B = 2	C = 3
4	A = 1	B = 3	C = 2	9	A = 3	B = 0	C = 1
5	A = 0	B = 3	C = 2	10	A = 3	B = 2	C = 0

4–10 points You have a small ecological footprint. You are doing well.

11–17 points You have a big ecological footprint. You need about one planet for your lifestyle.

18–30 points You have a huge ecological footprint. You need about three planets for your lifestyle!

Car ban

Language focus
giving opinions and persuading

Key vocabulary
environmental issues: *ban, car salesroom, congestion charge, traffic jam, tram*

Skills focus
reading: extracting key information
speaking: persuading

Level
upper-intermediate

Time
50 minutes

Preparation
one photocopy, cut up, for every 6 students

Warm-up

1. Ask the class who came to school by car. If the majority of your students come from families with cars, ask them to imagine how their lives would be different without a car. If they came mainly on foot or by public transport, ask them how their journey would change if they could drive themselves to school.
2. Depending on your town or city and how congested it is with traffic, ask some questions like *When was the last time you were in a traffic jam?* or *Do you think the public transport in our town is good?*

Main activity

1. Put students into groups of six and then divide the groups in half. Without letting them see the pictures in advance, give half the group Picture 1 and the other half Picture 2 and ask them to describe their picture to each other. This will naturally lead them to compare the two pictures when they've finished describing them.
2. Get feedback from the whole class. Ask prompt questions such as *Do you think a car-free city is possible? Why / Why not?*
3. Tell students they are going to take part in a meeting to discuss a possible car ban in the town in the picture full of cars. Draw a car in a circle with a cross through it to ensure students understand the word *ban.*
4. Give each member of the groups of six a role card A–F. Then re-group them so that all the As work together, all the Bs, etc. If you have a number of students that is not divisible by six, some groups can work in groups of five, leaving out any character apart from the mayor. In their new groups give students ten minutes to prepare their argument for or against the car ban. Be available to offer creative and linguistic support to the groups.
5. Now students return to their original group, with role cards A–F. Tell them they are at a meeting to discuss the pros and cons of the proposed car ban. They have to try and persuade the other members of their group to agree with them. Set a time limit of ten minutes for the meeting.
6. At the end of the task, ask each group to feed back on the success of their meeting and ask who was the most convincing.

Follow-up

- Giving students a second chance at the same or similar role-play is often a good idea. To add a new element to the activity the second time round, you could change the roles your students play and record them in action. Recording students will usually motivate them to do their best as they know that you, and the rest of the class, are going to listen to the recording at the end.
- Think about the students' own town, city or village. Have another discussion in groups of four to decide whether or not students would like to see a car ban in their town. This time the students can give their own opinions or students could think of four characters from the town and decide to be them.
- Ask students if they know anything about London's congestion charges and use the Internet to find out more. Ask students if they think this is a good idea.

17.3 Car ban

A You are the mayor of the city and you want to pass a new policy to ban cars from the city centre. You believe that the pollution from cars is the main reason for climate change and you want your city to set an example to the rest of the world. Your aim is to improve the public transport system and then introduce congestion charges so car drivers will have to pay a lot of money to come in to the city centre by car. Eventually you'd like to ban cars completely. You would like to eventually become an MP for the Green Party and you believe the car ban may be a step in the right direction for your political career.

B You live on the outskirts of the city and you have three children. You take them to school every day in your car. Their school is on the other side of the city. You can't imagine taking your children on the bus every day. The public transport in the city is overcrowded and unreliable. If the car ban takes place, you would have to change your children's school or move house so you could walk to school. You are so angry with the mayor of the city that you would even consider moving to another city without a car ban.

C You work as a courier and you spend your days cycling around the city. Bicycle is by far the quickest way to get around as the traffic is really bad. You think the car ban is an excellent idea as you've had several minor accidents on your bike recently and you fully believe that something must be done to make the city easier to move around in. At last your city has a mayor who wants to make real changes!

D You are a car salesman in the centre of the city and, of course, you think the mayor's plan is absolutely crazy! You believe that all big cities have traffic problems but people love their cars and won't change their habits. You are worried that if the mayor does impose a car ban you will have to close your car salesroom and move to another city.

E You love cars so much that you even belong to a 'tuning' club where you spend your weekends customising your cars. You think the mayor is crazy to propose a car ban and you can't imagine your weekends without being able to drive your car into the town centre. You don't believe that climate change is really happening and you're not worried about the environment. Life's too short!

F You've been a bus driver in the city for many years. The traffic has gradually got worse and it's making your job rather frustrating as you spend so much time in traffic. You believe that the mayor has a point and is right to take action to try and reduce the traffic congestion. However, before banning cars, you think the city has to invest a lot more in public transport. There aren't enough buses and the timetable needs to be extended so people can take buses at night. You also believe that a tram would be a good idea for your town.